# THE

# CLEAN VEGAN

## COOKBOOK

**60** Whole-Food, Plant-Based Recipes
to Nourish Your Body and Soul

# THE

# CLEAN VEGAN

## COOKBOOK

## JACKIE AKERBERG

Creator of Jackfruitful Kitchen

PAGE STREET
PUBLISHING CO.

PAGE STREET
PUBLISHING CO.

Copyright © 2023 Jackie Akerberg

First published in 2023 by
Page Street Publishing Co.
27 Congress Street, Suite 1511
Salem, MA 01970
www.pagestreetpublishing.com

Distributed by Macmillan, sales in Canada by The Canadian Manda Group.

27 26 25 24 23    1 2 3 4 5

ISBN-13: 978-1-64567-734-5
ISBN-10: 1-64567-734-6

Library of Congress Control Number: 2022942789

Cover and book design by Kylie Alexander for Page Street Publishing Co.
Photography by Jackie Akerberg

Printed and bound in the United States

# DEDICATION

To my loving parents, who first inspired my affinity for cooking with their incredible culinary skills, nightly family time in the kitchen and overall passion for delicious food and wine.

To my adoring husband, who always encourages me to pursue my passions, is my forever taste-tester and who originally encouraged me to go plant-based. I would not be where I am today without you, my love.

To my friends and family who have sampled dozens of recipes and provided thoughtful feedback.

And to my @jackfruitfulkitchen Insta-fam. This book would not have been possible without all of your support on my plant-based adventure. These recipes are for all of you!

# TABLE OF CONTENTS

## Balanced Breakfasts          107

## Sinless Sweets and Healthy Treats          133

# INTRODUCTION

Hi there, I'm Jackie! Many of you may know me from my Instagram @jackfruitfulkitchen, where I share colorful, unique, plant-based recipes designed to help you look and feel your best. I have always been a lover of healthy food, and while I've always included an abundance of plants in my diet, I decided to go fully plant-based and become vegan in 2019. This transition inspired me to start my Instagram account and blog.

I made the shift to eating a vegan diet for a number of reasons, including my love for animals and our oceans, my goal of helping protect our planet and the desire to feel my best by truly nourishing my body with the food I consume. Before going plant-based, I experienced digestive issues, challenges with my skin, severe allergies and asthma. By feeding my body clean, whole foods and nutrient-rich ingredients, I am happy to say I have never felt better and all of my prior health challenges have virtually disappeared. I can't wait for you to experience these nourishing recipes so you too can enjoy the power of a plant-based lifestyle.

At first blush, you may hear the word *vegan* and automatically assume a vegan diet must be healthy, but that's just not the case. In today's world, the word *vegan* means a lot of different things. You can be a raw vegan, a whole-food vegan and, nowadays, it's easier than ever to be a junk-food vegan! With more and more people transitioning to a plant-based diet or reducing their meat consumption, the market for vegan foods has grown immensely. An overly saturated market full of vegan products can be quite confusing for the consumer who is trying to eat a healthy, plant-based, nutrient-rich diet. Just remember this: Many of the most popular junk foods are unintentionally vegan. OREO® sandwich cookies, potato chips, white bread, a few flavors of DORITOS®, unfrosted varieties of Pop-Tarts® and many candies—all totally vegan! These foods, combined with so many new processed vegan foods hitting the market daily, means just eating vegan is no longer a direct path to healthy living.

Let's get real—this book is all about cutting the crap, being a *clean* vegan and enjoying every single minute of it. No plain carrot sticks or flavorless tofu here. These recipes are the real deal made with real, clean ingredients. Plus, we're going to have a lot of good, clean fun while making the recipes in this book—with no shortage of puns. The entire purpose of this book is to show you how fun a vegan lifestyle can be, how you can fuel your body with real food and how easy it is to ditch the processed ingredients. Pursuing a clean vegan diet is likely to give you more energy, improve your digestion, help support a healthy weight, reduce inflammation, improve your gut flora, boost your mood, reduce your cravings and help you feel amazing! And guess what? You don't have to compromise on deliciousness! I have poured my heart and soul into creating healthy, veganized versions of recipes you know and love, making them with only whole, nourishing ingredients.

The biggest changes I have made in how I cook and enjoy food since going vegan are using whole, organic foods, eliminating processed ingredients, cooking with little to no oil and cutting out processed grains and refined sugars. In this book, we save the oils for when it really counts, eliminating them in recipes where the same result can be achieved with whole ingredients. When you see a recipe without oil, this is to show you that you can in fact sauté, roast, make dressings and bake without it! That being said, if you love having cold-pressed organic oils in your life, then you can choose to use avocado or olive oil instead of water or vegetable broth.

Above all else, I have designed this book to be a fun read to help you simplify clean vegan eating and find meals you enjoy no matter what type of cuisine you are craving. Clean vegan eating should not feel restrictive or limited. My hope is for you to love these recipes and have them as your go-tos when you're craving something delicious. I have organized the book by meal type to make your meal planning for the week easier than ever and so that you can quickly find a delicious recipe for a balanced breakfast, a nourishing main, a superfood soup, a glowing bowl of greens or a sinless sweet and healthy treat. My main goal when writing this book was to share recipes with you that will have you exclaiming, "Wait, that's vegan *and* healthy?" I hope that with every bite of these recipes, you and your loved ones will experience that excitement while also feeling the benefits of these clean vegan recipes.

# VEGAN CLEAN–EATING ESSENTIALS

Whether you are a newcomer to the vegan diet or a seasoned veteran, the world of whole-food, vegan ingredients can be a bit intimidating. Especially when you aim to eat a *clean* plant-based diet, it can be hard to know which ingredients are must-haves and how to add clean and healthy flavor without the use of animal products and processed fats. In this section, I outline some essential ingredients that I always keep in my kitchen. I also share my favorite plant-based protein sources, because we all have heard (or asked) the question, "But where do you get your protein?" Bean there, done that! All you need to know about plant-based protein sources is included in these pages.

## Vegan Fridge and Pantry Staples

With so many plant-based ingredients out there, it can be overwhelming to stock a vegan kitchen. But romaine calm—I've got you covered! Having these items on hand and knowing when and how to use them will make healthy plant-based cooking as simple as can be.

### Almond, Cashew and Hazelnut Flours

These nut flours are low in carbs and full of nutrients and protein, making them great grain-free flour options. I use them in many of the recipes in this book. Please note, nut flours are typically not a 1:1 swap in most recipes.

### Apple Cider Vinegar

Apple cider vinegar has many nutritional properties and is also a fabulous tool for vegan baking. It adds a mild, tangy flavor, helps achieve a fluffier texture and can help activate baking soda.

### Applesauce

Unsweetened applesauce is used in many baked recipes in this book as a replacement for butter or oil. It also adds fiber to baked goods, provides natural sweetness and helps keep baked goods moist and fresh.

### Aquafaba

This magical substance is the liquid you find in a can of chickpeas. It is simply the water that has absorbed some of the chickpeas, and it is a wonderful thickening agent and egg substitute. I love using aquafaba as a substitute for egg whites in meringue-style recipes, whipped "cream" or anytime I want to add fluffiness to baked goods. While aquafaba's flavor is mild, it is noticeable in sweet recipes, so plan accordingly.

### Arrowroot Powder

Arrowroot powder is a starch extracted from the arrowroot plant. It is a great substitute for cornstarch and can be used as a thickener in many recipes. It is totally flavorless and odorless. This is a completely natural product that does not require high heat or chemicals in the production process. It is certified gluten-free, Paleo and kosher.

### Bragg® Liquid Aminos

Many people do not realize that traditional soy sauce is not gluten-free. If you do not need to avoid gluten, soy sauce is a perfectly fine option. If you are avoiding gluten, you can use Bragg Liquid Aminos, which is made by mixing hydrolyzed soybeans or fermented coconut sap with water, resulting in a naturally gluten-free product. This can be used interchangeably with soy sauce, coconut aminos and tamari; although, each has a slightly different flavor.

## Chickpea Flour

A wonderful egg substitute for use in omelets, quiches and more, chickpea flour is also a very versatile grain-free flour that can be used in both sweet and savory baked goods. It's a great source of fiber and protein.

## Coconut Aminos

Coconut aminos is a salty, savory seasoning sauce made from the fermented sap of coconut palms and sea salt. It is a wonderful alternative to soy sauce.

## Coconut Cream and Canned Full-Fat Coconut Milk

Canned coconut cream and canned full-fat coconut milk are great options for adding creaminess to vegan recipes. They will, however, add a slight coconutty flavor to dishes, so make sure to plan accordingly if you are experimenting with this ingredient in other recipes.

## Coconut Sugar

This granulated sweetener is a whole-food, plant-based unrefined sweetener that has a higher nutrient content and lower glycemic index than traditional sugar.

## Cold-Pressed Organic Avocado Oil

If you are choosing oil for roasting and sautéing, cold-pressed organic avocado oil is the way to go. The oil of the avocado is extracted by mashing and pressing, without the application of high heat. Avocado also has a much higher smoke point than olive oil, making it a healthier choice for roasting and sautéing at high temperatures.

## Cold-Pressed Organic Olive Oil

Instead of being processed with high heat, cold-pressed, organic olive oil is extracted through pressure, meaning that high levels of vitamin E, vitamin K and antioxidants, as well as other nutrients, are maintained in the finished product. Olive oil has a lower smoke point than avocado oil, so I typically enjoy it at room temperature on greens or drizzled on hummus.

## Dates

These nutrient powerhouses are used in many recipes in this book to add a natural sweetness, as well as fiber and antioxidants. Soft, high-quality Medjool dates are the best option for the recipes in this book. If your dates are too dry, simply soak them in hot water for a few minutes.

## Gluten-Free Rolled, Old-Fashioned or Steel-Cut Oats

While most oats are naturally gluten-free, if you are gluten-intolerant you will want to buy certified gluten-free oats. These are a great addition to so many recipes, both sweet and savory, and rolled oats can even be made into a quick and easy flour.

## Gluten-Free Vegan Bread

Often, gluten-free breads contain eggs in the ingredients, so be sure to read labels, or flip to page 131 for my Get Up and Go Super Seed Bread.

## Grain-Free Pasta

Many pasta shapes are now made entirely from chickpeas or lentils and pair perfectly with the pasta recipes in this book.

## Grain-Free Tortillas

Any type of tortilla can be used in my recipes, but my favorite options are tortillas made from almond flour or cassava flour. They have a fabulous texture, boast great flavor and are higher in protein and lower in carbs than traditional tortillas.

## Ground Flaxseed

Ground flaxseed is my favorite egg replacer for baked goods. Combine 1 tablespoon (7 g) of ground flaxseed with 3 tablespoons (45 ml) of water and let the mixture sit for 10 to 15 minutes. The mixture will become slightly gelatinous and results in the perfect one-to-one substitute for eggs. Flaxseed is also a fabulous source of fiber and protein.

## Jackfruit

Young green jackfruit is a wonderful plant-based meat alternative that has a very similar texture to shredded chicken or pulled pork and an almost indiscernible flavor. It is very different when harvested young, as once it is ripe it has a much sweeter taste similar to mango or pineapple. For every recipe in this book that calls for jackfruit, you will want to use young green jackfruit, which is most commonly found in canned or frozen varieties.

## Kala Namak

This Indian salt has a sulfur-like aroma and is used to add an eggy taste to vegan omelets and tofu scrambles. Sea salt can always be used instead. Some grocery stores, especially specialty stores and ethnic food stores, will carry this type of salt; otherwise, there are multiple brands you can order online.

## Maple Syrup

Pure grade A or grade B maple syrup is a wonderful whole-food, plant-based sweetener that is a much healthier alternative to refined sugar. It is full of essential minerals and powerful antioxidants.

## Miso Paste

Miso paste is a wonderful way to add a cheesy umami flavor to dressings, soups and sauces. It is made from fermented soybeans.

## Nutritional Yeast

Used to add a cheesy flavor to many vegan recipes, nutritional yeast is also a great source of vitamins—like vitamin B12—and minerals. Nutritional yeast can be found in the baking aisle or spice aisle at most grocery stores, and it's readily available online.

## Oat Flour

This is a fabulous single-ingredient, gluten-free flour that is full of protein, fiber and minerals. Out of all gluten-free flours, oat flour performs most similarly to traditional all-purpose or whole-wheat flour.

## Plant Milk

Not only are plant-based milks healthier for you but they are also much better for our planet. When recipes in this book call for plant milk, you can use plain unsweetened almond, soy, cashew or oat milk.

## Raw Cacao Powder

Raw cacao powder is the raw, unsweetened version of cocoa. The main difference between raw cacao powder and cocoa powder, other than it being unsweetened, is that it is not processed at a high temperature. This means that the powerful nutrients and antioxidants are preserved. Raw cacao powder can be used in any recipe in place of cocoa powder.

## Raw Cashews

Raw cashews are used in many recipes in this book to create creaminess in both savory and sweet dishes. If you do not have a high-speed blender, you will need to soak raw cashews overnight or boil them for 10 minutes before blending them.

## Tahini

Also known as sesame seed paste, tahini is used in many recipes throughout this book. Different brands of tahini can vary greatly in texture and taste, so be sure to seek out a variety that is runny in texture and not too bitter. Some types of tahini can have the texture of concrete and a very bitter taste, and those varieties are best avoided.

## Tamari

Tamari is most similar to soy sauce and is naturally free of wheat and gluten, but it is still made from fermented soybeans. It is also slightly higher in protein than soy sauce and contains healthy antioxidants.

## Tapioca Flour

Tapioca flour is a starch derived from the cassava root, which is a root vegetable. This starch is a great thickening agent and substitute for cornstarch in sauces, baked goods, soups and more.

## Unrefined Coconut Butter

Unlike coconut oil, which is a processed food made up of almost entirely saturated fat, coconut butter is a whole food made from whole coconut, so it has many more nutrients than coconut oil. Coconut butter also includes fiber, which is absent in coconut oil. In addition, coconut butter has a richer, creamier texture and taste. You always have the option of substituting coconut oil for any recipe in this book that uses coconut butter.

## Vegan Yogurt

Vegan yogurt can be a much healthier option than traditional dairy-based yogurt. For recipes in this book, look for plain, unsweetened plant-based yogurts made from coconut, cashews or almonds. Greek-style yogurts with a thicker, creamier texture work best.

## Whole-Grain, Gluten-Free Pasta

If you're not avoiding grains, look for pasta made from brown rice, corn or millet.

## Vegan Protein Sources

One of the most common questions vegans receive has to be, "How do you get protein?" Thankfully, it is actually quite simple to consume the necessary amount of protein on a plant-based diet, and this section will tell you about some of the best sources of protein in the plant world.

## Beans

Beans such as pinto beans, black beans, chickpeas and cannellini beans are incredibly high in fiber, which helps keep you full and satisfied for a long period of time. Along with being high in fiber and various nutrients, they also have about 15 grams of protein per 1-cup (172-g) serving.

## Edamame

Edamame is merely young soybeans. Edamame can be served raw, steamed, boiled or sautéed. There are 17 grams of protein in 1 cup (155 g) of edamame.

## Lentils

Lentils are a fabulous source of protein, fiber, vitamins and minerals. Each 1-cup (198-g) serving of cooked lentils contains 18 grams of protein. There are various types of lentils, including green, red, brown, yellow and black.

## Nuts

On average, nuts have anywhere from 10 to 27 grams of protein per 1-cup (143-g) serving, along with many essential vitamins, minerals and healthy fats. I recommend purchasing raw, unsalted nuts for the cleanest option and avoiding varieties that are salted or sweetened. Throughout this book, you will find recipes with instructions on roasting a variety of raw nuts at home, and you can even find instructions for making candied walnuts on page 95.

## Oatmeal

Oatmeal is a great source of plant protein, with 1 cup (90 g) of rolled oats containing about 6 grams of protein and 1 cup (161 g) of steel-cut oats boasting 21 grams of protein.

## Peas

Green peas are a surprisingly great source of plant protein! Each 1-cup (134-g) serving contains 8 grams of protein.

## Quinoa

Quinoa is an amazing plant protein source because it contains all nine essential amino acids. Three colors of quinoa are widely available: white, red and black. Tricolor quinoa is a mixture of all three colors. 1 cup (185 g) of cooked quinoa contains 8 grams of protein.

## Seeds

Seeds are a wonderful source of vitamins and minerals. Hemp seeds have the highest protein content of any seed, with just 1 tablespoon (10 g) boasting a little more than 3 grams of protein. Seeds are also rich in fiber and healthy fats. The other seeds with the greatest amount of protein per 1-tablespoon (15-g) serving are pumpkin (3 g), sunflower (2 g), chia (2 g) and flax (1 g).

## Silken Tofu

The only difference between silken tofu and regular tofu is that the soy milk is coagulated versus curdled, and it is left entirely unpressed, giving it a wonderfully soft, smooth and silky texture. Silken tofu is a great option if you want to add protein to smoothies, sauces, soups, dips and more. A 4-ounce (113-g) serving of silken tofu has nearly 8 grams of protein.

## Tempeh

Tempeh is similar to tofu in that it is made from soybeans, but it is much firmer, nuttier, denser and meatier in texture. It is made from soybeans that have been fermented and then compressed. A 4-ounce (113-g) serving of tempeh contains nearly 21 grams of protein.

## Tofu

Tofu is a nutrient-rich plant protein source that is low in calories and fat, contains zero cholesterol and has very few carbs. It also contains high levels of many essential vitamins and minerals, including calcium, manganese, copper, selenium, vitamin A, iron, magnesium and zinc. Tofu is traditionally made from organic soybeans, making it a fabulous minimally processed food. There are various types of tofu differentiated by firmness, and the only difference is the amount of water used to produce the tofu. Super firm tofu has the lowest water content, producing a firmer, meatier texture. It's the best option for pan-searing and grilling. Firm and extra firm tofu are best for marinating, baking and scrambling. A 4-ounce (113-g) serving of tofu contains almost 18 grams of protein. Note that in recipes that produce a crispy, firm and meaty tofu, I find that super firm tofu is the best option. It is also great for times when you are looking for a quick and easy meal, because it doesn't need to be pressed. Whenever you see pressed tofu in a list of ingredients, you can use super firm tofu if you prefer to totally bypass the pressing step.

# NOURISHING MAINS

Mains! The dishes that make up the biggest and best meal of the day, the time we most often gather as a family and the meal we most frequently host for friends. I love this chapter because it truly shows that the dinner parties you love hosting, the meals you have with family and the plates you cozy up to at the end of long workdays do not have to be lackluster when you follow a clean and healthy plant-based lifestyle. That's right, this chapter is full of crave-worthy, hearty, nourishing dishes that are bursting with ex-soy-lent flavor. Also, each recipe in this chapter just so happens to make an incredibly stunning plate, which is always easier to create when you're eating an abundance of plants.

This chapter has it all. It kicks off with the Best Ever Veggie Burgers (page 18), and trust me when I say they were given that name for a reason. The culinary adventure continues with dishes inspired by various cuisines, including Asian, Italian, Indian and Greek. You will find recognizable favorites here, like Bolognese pasta, flatbread pizza, tacos and even mac and cheese, each dish more nourishing than its traditional counterpart. This chapter was written with the entire family in mind, and each recipe can be enjoyed by even the pickiest of eaters.

My personal favorite in this chapter is the Tasty-as-Takeout Teriyaki Cauliflower Bowls (page 36), so if you're looking for somewhere to start your journey through these pages, there's no better place. I hope you get lost in these pages, marking many recipes to try and adding them to your regular rotation of weeknight meals. I want them to become staple recipes in the heart of your home, nourishing the bodies and souls of you and your loved ones.

## Quick Pickled Onions

1 large red onion, sliced into rings ⅛" (3 mm) thick

2 tbsp (30 ml) fresh or refrigerated orange juice

Juice of 1 large lemon

Juice of 1 large lime

2 tbsp (30 ml) apple cider vinegar

¼ tsp salt

## Veggie Burgers

Water, vegetable broth or avocado oil, as needed

½ small red onion, coarsely chopped

2 cloves garlic, minced

¾ cup (53 g) cremini mushrooms, coarsely chopped

1 small carrot, grated

1 cup (164 g) canned chickpeas, drained

½ cup (45 g) gluten-free rolled oats

2 tbsp (12 g) gluten-free oat flour, plus more as needed

2 tbsp (14 g) ground flaxseed

1½ tbsp (24 g) tomato paste

1 tsp ground cumin

½ tsp ground coriander

1 tsp paprika

1 tsp chili powder

½ tsp salt

½ tsp black pepper

2 tbsp (30 ml) coconut aminos, Bragg Liquid Aminos, soy sauce or tamari

# BEST EVER VEGGIE BURGERS

### Yields 8 burgers

Burgers are at the heart of every summer barbecue, and eating plant-based doesn't mean you have to miss out. The vegan market is saturated with processed artificial meats, so finding a solid veggie burger made from real, whole ingredients can be a true challenge. I'm going to speak on behalf of vegans far and wide and say that what we want in our burger is great texture, lots of veggies, natural plant protein and a killer sauce that brings it all together. Am I right? Well, after years of perfecting this recipe, I couldn't be more excited to tell you: This veggie burger is bun in a million. Its texture is firm enough to stand up to the grill, and it can absolutely hold its own on a bun. Trust me when I say that this veggie burger is the only burger recipe you need. Happy grilling!

Begin by making the quick pickled onions ahead of time. In a large jar, combine the onion slices, orange juice, lemon juice, lime juice, vinegar and salt. Securely tighten the lid of the jar and shake it vigorously. Chill the onions in the fridge for at least 2 hours, or preferably overnight. Store the pickled onions in an airtight container in the fridge for up to 4 weeks (see Tip on page 20).

To make the veggie burgers, preheat the oven to 400°F (204°C). Line a large baking sheet with parchment paper.

While the oven is preheating, heat a large cast-iron skillet over medium heat and add about 1 tablespoon (15 ml) of water. Add the onion and garlic and sauté them for 2 to 3 minutes, until the onion is slightly tender and fragrant. Add the mushrooms and carrot and sauté the mixture for 3 to 4 minutes, until the veggies are crisp-tender. You may need to add a little more water to deglaze the skillet as the veggies are cooking. Remove the skillet from the heat and let the veggies cool for about 5 minutes.

Transfer the veggie mixture to a food processor. Add the chickpeas, oats, oat flour, flaxseed, tomato paste, cumin, coriander, paprika, chili powder, salt, black pepper and coconut aminos. Pulse the ingredients eight to ten times, until they are well combined but not pureed. Scrape down the sides of the food processor between pulses if needed. The mixture should be a doughy texture with some chunkiness retained from the vegetables and chickpeas. If the mixture is a little too wet to the touch, add additional oat flour 1 tablespoon (6 g) at a time.

Divide the mixture into eight even portions. Create the patties by rolling each section into a ball and flattening it between your palms. Place each patty on the prepared baking sheet, spaced 1½ inches (4 cm) apart.

(continued)

### Classic Burger Sauce

½ cup (120 ml) plain unsweetened vegan Greek yogurt

4 tsp (20 ml) Sriracha or chili-garlic sauce, or to taste

1 tbsp (15 ml) Dijon mustard, or to taste

### Must-Have Burger Toppings

8 gluten-free burger buns

8 leaves butter lettuce

2–3 large Roma tomatoes, thinly sliced

1 large avocado, mashed

¼ cup (29 g) Quick Pickled Onions

¼ cup (6 g) microgreens

Cornichons or spicy pickles, for serving

Bake the burgers for 30 minutes, flipping them halfway through the baking time.

While the burgers are baking, prepare the classic burger sauce. In a medium jar, combine the yogurt, Sriracha and mustard. Use a fork to whisk the ingredients together. Taste the sauce and adjust the spiciness with extra Sriracha or the tang with extra mustard.

To prepare the must-have burger toppings, place the burger buns on a large baking sheet and warm them in the oven for the final 2 minutes of the burgers' baking time. Alternatively, you may place the buns directly on the oven rack to warm them. Assemble your burgers by layering the buns with the lettuce, tomatoes, avocado, quick pickled onions, a burger patty, the classic burger sauce and microgreens. Serve the burgers with the cornichons on the side.

Any leftover burgers can be frozen, stored in a reusable bag or container, for up to 6 months. To reheat the burgers, thaw them and reheat them in a skillet over low heat for 2 to 3 minutes per side. Alternatively, you can grill the leftover burgers over low heat on lightly oiled grates or a lightly oiled piece of aluminum foil for 2 to 3 minutes per side.

TIP: Enjoy my pickled onions on top of tacos, burgers, salads, curries and more for a burst of bright and tangy flavor.

## Cauliflower Steaks

1 large head cauliflower

1 tbsp (15 ml) coconut aminos, Bragg Liquid Aminos, soy sauce or tamari

½ tsp salt, plus more as needed

½ tsp black pepper, plus more as needed

½ tsp garlic powder

½ tsp paprika

1 tbsp (11 g) nutritional yeast

2 cups (480 ml) water

½ cup (96 g) black lentils

2 tbsp (30 ml) balsamic vinegar

Water, vegetable broth or avocado oil, as needed

8 oz (224 g) cremini mushrooms, thinly sliced

2 tbsp (14 g) coarsely chopped pecans

4 cups (120 g) baby spinach

# CAULIFLOWER STEAKS WITH BALSAMIC BLACK LENTILS AND LEMONY TAHINI

### Yields 4 servings

Eating plant-based is simple as can be when you love a wide variety of cuisines. When you think about creating a traditional, American-style meal that consists of a vegetable, a starchy carb and a protein (typically a meat), you need a little more creativity. This is that meal. The cauliflower is the star of the show with its perfectly tender yet meaty texture, and it is accompanied by protein-packed lentils, nutritious supporting veggies and a lemon-tahini sauce that is to die for. This dish embodies that satiating umami flavor that meat eaters know and love. It is a dish that will please the entire room, no matter the diners' dietary preferences.

To make the cauliflower steaks, preheat the oven to 500°F (260°C). Line a large baking sheet with aluminum foil.

Place the head of cauliflower right side up on a cutting board. Slice directly down the middle to cut it in half. Find the place where the leaves begin on the stem and make a cut at that point to remove the leaves and lower portion of the stem, keeping the rest of the cauliflower head intact. Set the cauliflower halves right side up and, slicing in 1-inch (2.5-cm)-thick sections from top to bottom, create four cauliflower steaks. Set aside any small pieces to save for another recipe.

Place the cauliflower steaks on the prepared baking sheet. Evenly brush each side of the steaks with the coconut aminos.

In a small bowl, thoroughly combine the salt, black pepper, garlic powder, paprika and nutritional yeast. Sprinkle the seasoning mixture on both sides of the steaks and gently rub them to coat them with the seasoning.

Cover the baking sheet with aluminum foil. Bake the cauliflower steaks for 5 minutes. Remove the foil and bake the steaks for 8 minutes. Flip the steaks and bake them for another 8 minutes.

While the cauliflower is baking, fill a small saucepan with the water and bring it to a boil over high heat. Add the lentils and reduce the heat to low. Simmer the lentils for 12 minutes, until they are tender but not mushy. Drain the lentils and return them to the saucepan. Stir in the vinegar.

While the lentils are cooking, heat a large cast-iron skillet over medium-high heat. Add a small amount of water and swirl the skillet to coat it. Add the mushrooms and sauté them for 5 to 7 minutes, until they are golden brown. Season them with a pinch of salt and a pinch of black pepper. Stir in the pecans and cook the mixture for 1 to 2 minutes to toast the nuts. Add the spinach and sauté the mixture for 2 to 3 minutes, until the spinach has wilted.

(continued)

### Lemony Tahini

3 tbsp (45 ml) runny tahini

Juice of 1 large lemon

½ tsp garlic powder

2 tsp (10 ml) pure maple syrup

Pinch of salt

Pinch of black pepper

1–4 tbsp (15–60 ml) water (optional)

¼ cup (15 g) fresh parsley, finely chopped, for garnish

To make the lemony tahini, mix together the tahini, lemon juice, garlic powder, maple syrup, salt and black pepper in a small bowl. Depending on the consistency of your tahini, you can add 1 tablespoon (15 ml) of water at a time until your desired thickness is reached.

Drizzle the tahini sauce on four serving plates. Arrange the balsamic lentils on each plate on top of the sauce. Top the lentils with the cauliflower steaks. Finally, add the sautéed mushrooms, pecans and spinach. Garnish each serving with the parsley.

## Tempeh Filling

Water, vegetable broth or avocado oil, as needed

8 oz (224 g) tempeh, crumbled into very small pieces

4 cloves garlic, minced

2 tbsp (28 g) minced fresh ginger

2 medium carrots, shredded

## Sweet and Tangy Orange Sauce

½ cup (120 ml) fresh orange juice

2 tbsp (12 g) orange zest

¼ cup (60 ml) water

1 tbsp (15 ml) chili-garlic sauce

3 tbsp (45 ml) unseasoned rice vinegar

2 tbsp (30 ml) coconut aminos, Bragg Liquid Aminos, soy sauce or tamari

3 tbsp (45 ml) pure maple syrup

1½ tsp (5 g) tapioca flour or arrowroot powder

## Lettuce Wraps

8 oz (224 g) whole-grain or heart of palm noodles, cooked

12–16 lettuce leaves (such as iceberg, romaine or butter lettuce)

2 green onions, finely chopped, for garnish

¼ cup (18 g) finely shredded red cabbage, for garnish

2 large limes, sliced into wedges

# SWEET AND SPICY ORANGE TEMPEH LETTUCE WRAPS

## Yields 12 to 16 lettuce wraps

When I was a kid, one of my favorite things to order at a Chinese restaurant was orange chicken, but I always told my parents, "I wish they made it without chicken." At your average restaurant in the '90s, that wasn't happening! However, times have changed—I have a new spin on that perfectly sweet and tangy classic orange sauce we all know and love, but without the refined sugar or oil. Orange you glad? You can use this sauce in veggie stir-fries, on cauliflower wings or in these tempeh lettuce wraps. The tender tempeh is simmered in the flavorful sauce for a meaty, power-packed filling inside a tender lettuce leaf. This dish is loaded with protein and delicious flavor that I know you will love just as much—if not more—than traditional takeout.

To prepare the tempeh filling, heat a large cast-iron skillet over medium heat. Add enough water to lightly coat the bottom of the skillet. Add the tempeh to the skillet in an even layer and cook it, undisturbed, for 2 to 3 minutes, adding a small amount of additional water to deglaze the skillet if needed. Stir the tempeh and repeat, letting the tempeh cook on the opposite side for 2 to 3 minutes, until it begins to brown.

While the tempeh is cooking, make the sweet and tangy orange sauce. In a medium jar, whisk together the orange juice, orange zest, water, chili-garlic sauce, vinegar, coconut aminos, maple syrup and tapioca flour. Set the jar of sauce aside.

When the tempeh is golden, add another splash of water, then add the garlic, ginger and carrots. Sauté the mixture for 1 to 2 minutes, until the garlic and ginger are fragrant and the carrot is tender. Pour the sauce into the skillet and bring the mixture to a gentle simmer, stirring it occasionally. Reduce the heat to medium-low and cook the orange tempeh for 2 to 3 minutes, stirring it frequently, until the sauce has thickened and the tempeh is coated and glossy.

Assemble the lettuce wraps by dividing the noodles among the lettuce leaves and topping each wrap with the tempeh filling. Garnish each wrap with a sprinkle of green onions and shredded cabbage. Squeeze the lime wedges over the lettuce wraps and serve.

12 oz (336 g) lentil linguine

6 large kale leaves

2 cups (60 g) loosely packed baby spinach

3 tbsp (45 ml) fresh lemon juice

2 cloves garlic

¼ cup (44 g) nutritional yeast

1 tsp salt, plus more as needed

1 tsp black pepper, plus more as needed

¼ cup (15 g) fresh parsley, plus more for garnish

⅓ cup (49 g) raw cashews

1 tbsp (17 g) white miso

1 tsp pure maple syrup

# SUPER GREENS GODDESS PASTA

## Yields 4 servings

Can you really have creamy pasta that will nourish your body and make you feel like a goddess? You bet. This oil-free recipe is the pasta of your dreams. It's incredibly creamy with cheesy flavor, but it is secretly full of superfoods and veggies, meaning you really can have your cake and eat it too. This health-supporting sauce is delightful on any noodle you choose, but I pair it with a lentil-based linguine, which adds an abundance of fiber, folate, iron, potassium and protein.

Bring a large pot of water to a boil over high heat. Add the linguine. Cook the pasta according to the package's directions (see Tip). While the linguine is boiling, add the kale leaves to the water and allow them to boil for 1 to 2 minutes, until they turn a vibrant dark green color. Remove the kale leaves from the water, letting excess water drip off them.

Transfer the kale to a high-speed blender. Add the spinach, lemon juice, garlic, nutritional yeast, salt, black pepper, parsley, cashews, miso, maple syrup and ½ cup (120 ml) of the pasta water. Blend the ingredients for 60 to 90 seconds, until the sauce is completely smooth and creamy. Season the sauce with additional salt and black pepper if desired.

When the pasta is al dente, drain it and return it to the pot. Pour the goddess sauce over the noodles and quickly toss to combine. Transfer the pasta to serving bowls and top each serving with additional parsley.

Any leftover sauce can be kept in the fridge for up to 1 week or in the freezer for up to 6 months. Reheated sauce should be added to the pasta right before serving.

TIP: I find that with many lentil- or chickpea-based pastas, cooking the pasta for 1 to 2 minutes fewer than recommended on the package often achieves the best results, so check your pasta for doneness early and often.

## Falafel

3 cloves garlic

2 green onions

1 cup (60 g) loosely packed parsley

½ cup (8 g) loosely packed cilantro

1 tsp salt

½ tsp black pepper

½ tsp ground turmeric

1 tsp ground cumin

1 tsp paprika

¼ cup (28 g) ground flaxseed

1 (14-oz [392-g]) can chickpeas, drained, 2 tbsp (30 ml) aquafaba reserved

¼ cup (23 g) chickpea flour, plus more as needed

1 tbsp (10 g) whole golden flaxseed

1 tbsp (10 g) hemp seeds

1 tbsp (9 g) white sesame seeds

1 tbsp (9 g) black sesame seeds

## Bowls

1 cup (170 g) dry white quinoa

1 small head romaine lettuce, coarsely chopped

2 large Roma tomatoes, coarsely chopped

1 large English cucumber, thinly sliced

## Cool Cucumber Tzatziki

1 cup (240 ml) plain unsweetened vegan Greek yogurt

½ tsp garlic powder

¼ cup (13 g) finely chopped dill

2 tbsp (30 ml) fresh lime juice

Pinch of salt and black pepper

½ cup (133 g) grated English cucumber

¼ cup finely chopped fresh cilantro leaves, for garnish

# SUPER SEED FALAFEL BOWLS WITH COOL CUCUMBER TZATZIKI

## Yields 4 servings

Falafel is one of those foods that is naturally full of flavor, loaded with incredibly zesty herbs and spices and packed with plant protein. Basically a vegan's dream, right? Well, falafel at restaurants often contain both egg and gluten, and they are almost always deep-fried, turning this power-packed Mediterranean gem into something that isn't so healthy after all. My recipe is baked, not fried, contains no gluten or animal products and does not compromise on flavor, meaning there's nothing to falafel about! Plus, these falafel are rolled in protein-packed seeds for extra nutrients and fiber! They are perfect on these fresh and flavorful veggie bowls, but they're also delicious in wraps.

To make the falafel, preheat the oven to 375°F (191°C). Line a large baking sheet with parchment paper.

In a food processor, combine the garlic, green onions, parsley, cilantro, salt, black pepper, turmeric, cumin and paprika. Process the ingredients until they are well combined. Add the ground flaxseed, chickpeas, aquafaba and flour. Pulse the ingredients until they are combined but not pureed. It is very important to not puree the mixture, or it will be overly soggy and wet. Some chunkiness is ideal. If the mixture feels a little too moist, add an additional tablespoon (6 g) of flour.

In a small bowl, use a fork or spoon to combine the whole flaxseed, hemp seeds, white sesame seeds and black sesame seeds. Scoop out 1½ tablespoons (23 g) of the mixture, and then use your hands to roll the falafel mixture into a ball. Roll the falafel ball in the seed mixture to coat it. Place the falafel ball on the prepared baking sheet. Repeat this process until you have formed and coated twenty falafel balls, making sure to space the balls about 2 inches (5 cm) apart on the baking sheet. Bake the falafel for 25 to 30 minutes, until they are lightly golden and firm to the touch.

While the falafel are baking, begin preparing the bowls. Cook the quinoa according to the package's directions.

While the quinoa is cooking, prepare the cool cucumber tzatziki. In a small bowl, stir together the yogurt, garlic powder, dill, lime juice, salt and black pepper. Wrap the grated cucumber in a clean kitchen towel and squeeze out as much moisture as possible. Add the cucumber to the yogurt mixture and season the tzatziki with more lime juice, salt and black pepper if desired.

Assemble the bowls by placing a bed of lettuce in the bottom of each bowl and topping the lettuce with the tomatoes, quinoa, cucumber and falafel. Drizzle each serving with the cool cucumber tzatziki sauce and garnish each with the cilantro.

## Ground "Beef"

1 medium red onion, quartered

3 cloves garlic

8 oz (224 g) cremini mushrooms

8 oz (224 g) tempeh

¾ cup (75 g) walnuts

Water, vegetable broth or avocado oil, as needed

1 tbsp (8 g) chili powder

2 tsp (4 g) ground cumin

¼ tsp cayenne, plus more as needed

1 tsp salt

½ tsp black pepper

1 tsp paprika

½ tsp dried oregano

½ tsp ground coriander

2 tbsp (30 ml) coconut aminos, Bragg Liquid Aminos, soy sauce or tamari

3 tbsp (48 g) tomato paste

¼ cup (60 ml) water

## Tacos

12 (6 or 8" [15- or 20-cm]) soft almond flour tortillas

1 cup (172 g) canned black beans, warmed

1 large avocado, thinly sliced

1 cup (149 g) cherry tomatoes, quartered

¼ cup (29 g) Quick Pickled Onions (page 18)

¼ cup (4 g) finely chopped fresh cilantro leaves

¼ cup (18 g) shredded red cabbage

½ cup (120 ml) salsa (optional)

½ cup (120 ml) plain unsweetened vegan Greek yogurt (optional)

# GROUND "BEEF" TEX-MEX TACOS

## Yields 4 servings

No beef here! Let's taco 'bout it—if you grew up in the United States, chances are ground beef tacos were a part of your childhood. Perhaps they were a very fond part of your childhood. Well, a clean and healthy plant-based lifestyle doesn't mean you can't enjoy your favorite classic American tacos. This Tex-Mex-inspired taco meat is made from nutrient-rich mushrooms, tempeh and walnuts and is accompanied by flavorful spices and bright, delicious toppings. A grain-free tortilla is the perfect carrier, but if you'd like to increase your veggie intake even more, this taco meat is also delicious layered on top of a taco salad! You will be instantly transported back to your childhood taco memories with every bite.

To make the ground "beef," place the red onion and garlic in a food processor and pulse them six times, until they are finely diced. Transfer the onion-garlic mixture to a small bowl and set it aside. Place the mushrooms and tempeh in the food processor and pulse them eight times, until they are minced. Add the mushroom-tempeh mixture to the bowl with the onions and garlic. Add the walnuts to the food processor and pulse them about twelve times, until they are finely chopped.

Heat a large cast-iron skillet over medium heat. Add a small amount of water to coat the skillet. Add the diced vegetable-tempeh mixture and sauté it for 3 to 4 minutes, until the veggies are tender, adding more water or broth 1 tablespoon (15 ml) at a time to deglaze the skillet if needed.

Add the walnuts to the skillet and sauté the mixture for 2 to 3 minutes. Add the chili powder, cumin, cayenne, salt, black pepper, paprika, oregano and coriander. Stir the mixture to thoroughly combine it with the spices and cook it for 30 seconds. Stir in the coconut aminos, tomato paste and water. Bring the ground "beef" to a gentle simmer and cook it for 4 to 5 minutes, until the liquid is absorbed and the mixture has thickened. Season the ground "beef" with additional cayenne if desired.

While the ground "beef" is cooking, begin preparing the tortillas. Preheat the oven to 250°F (121°C). Heat a small skillet over medium-low heat and warm the tortillas one at a time in the skillet for about 30 seconds on each side, until they are slightly golden. Place the tortillas in the preheated oven to keep them warm.

To assemble the tacos, fill each tortilla with the ground "beef" and black beans, and top them with the avocado, cherry tomatoes, Quick Pickled Onions, cilantro, red cabbage, salsa (if using) and yogurt (if using).

Any leftover ground "beef" can be stored in a reusable bag or container for up to 5 days in the fridge, or frozen for up to 6 months. Thaw the "beef" in the microwave or in a skillet over low heat for easy weeknight fiestas.

## YELLOW CURRY CAULIFLOWER FRIED RICE WITH PINEAPPLE AND CASHEWS

### Yields 4 servings

Caul-it what you want, this recipe is delicious! Cauliflower rice can get a bad rap for being bland or mushy, but that is not the case with this recipe. It is a fun curried spin on traditional fried rice and is hearty enough to be your main course for an easy low-carb, high-protein weeknight dinner. I especially love to make this recipe for people who think they don't love cauliflower rice. Their minds are instantly changed, and yours will be too!

12 oz (336 g) extra firm tofu, pressed (see Tip) and cut into 1" (2.5-cm) cubes

3 tbsp (45 ml) coconut aminos, divided

Water, vegetable broth or avocado oil, as needed

4 green onions, finely chopped, white and green parts divided

2 cloves garlic, minced

1 tbsp (14 g) minced fresh ginger

1 medium red bell pepper, finely chopped

1 large carrot, grated

1 tbsp (6 g) curry powder

1 tsp ground turmeric

1 tsp ground cumin

1 tsp paprika

½ tsp salt

1 tsp chili-garlic sauce

7 cups (791 g) fresh or frozen cauliflower rice

1 cup (134 g) frozen green peas, thawed

1 cup (165 g) cubed fresh pineapple

½ cup (73 g) roasted unsalted cashews, coarsely chopped

1 large lime, sliced, for serving

Preheat the oven to 400°F (204°C). Line a large baking sheet with parchment paper.

Place the tofu cubes in a large bowl. Add 1 tablespoon (15 ml) of the coconut aminos and toss the tofu to coat the cubes. Spread the tofu cubes evenly on the prepared baking sheet. Bake the tofu for 15 minutes. Use a metal spatula to flip the tofu, and then bake it for 10 minutes, or until your desired crispiness is reached.

While the tofu is baking, heat a large cast-iron skillet or wok over medium heat. Add a small amount of water to coat the bottom of the skillet. Add the white portions of the green onions, garlic and ginger and sauté them for 1 to 2 minutes, until they are fragrant. Add the bell pepper and carrot and sauté the veggies for 30 seconds. Add the curry powder, turmeric, cumin, paprika, salt, remaining 2 tablespoons (30 ml) of coconut aminos and chili-garlic sauce. Sauté the spiced veggie mixture for 30 seconds. Add the cauliflower rice and stir the ingredients well, coating the cauliflower evenly with the spices and sauce.

Reduce the heat to medium-low and cook the cauliflower rice for 3 to 4 minutes, stirring it only every 60 seconds so that the cauliflower sears on each side. When the cauliflower is tender but not mushy, stir in the green peas, pineapple and cashews, and then cook the rice for 1 minute, until everything is heated through.

Remove the tofu from the oven and gently fold it into the fried rice. Serve the fried rice hot topped with the greens of the green onions and the lime.

TIP: My preferred way of pressing tofu may be a bit different than what you're used to! First, stand the tofu up on its side and slice it vertically into three ¾-inch (2-cm)-thick slabs. Place the three slabs on a clean kitchen towel, and fold the towel over to cover the tofu. Top the wrapped tofu with a cutting board, and then place something heavy like a large Dutch oven, a few cans or a heavy-bottomed skillet on top of the cutting board to press the tofu for 10 minutes.

Avocado oil spray

1 small sweet potato, peeled and cut into 1" (2.5-cm) cubes

1 cup (100 g) frozen cauliflower florets

⅔ cup (97 g) raw cashews

2 cloves garlic

12 oz (336 g) lentil rigatoni

1 cup (240 ml) water

Juice of ½ small lemon

1 tbsp (15 ml) coconut aminos, Bragg Liquid Aminos, soy sauce or tamari

2 tsp (10 ml) Dijon mustard

⅓ cup (59 g) nutritional yeast

2 tbsp (34 g) white miso

1 tsp onion powder

1 tsp paprika or smoked paprika

½ tsp ground turmeric

1 tsp salt, plus more as needed

½ tsp black pepper

2 tbsp (18 g) tapioca flour

¼ cup (27 g) cauliflower bread crumbs or ¼ cup (21 g) almond meal

# SIMPLE BAKED MAC AND CHEESE

## Yields 6 servings

This mac and cheese delivers. Just what does it deliver? Creaminess, coziness and an abundance of veggies! It is going to mac you smile with the same comforting flavor of your favorite mac and cheese, but without any animal products, unhealthy fats or processed artificial cheeses. This recipe pairs a perfect balance of salty, savory flavor with an unbelievable creaminess created by the sweet potato, cauliflower and cashews. This bowl will have you exclaiming, "I can't believe it's not cheese!"

Preheat the oven to 350°F (177°C). Lightly spray one 8-inch (20-cm) round baking dish with avocado oil spray.

Fill a medium saucepan two-thirds full of water and bring it to a boil over high heat. Add the sweet potato, cauliflower, cashews and garlic. Reduce the heat to medium and gently boil the ingredients for 12 minutes, until the sweet potatoes and cauliflower are fork-tender. Drain the ingredients using a colander and let them cool for 1 to 2 minutes in the colander. Immediately refill the saucepan with water and bring it to a boil over high heat to prepare the rigatoni. Add the pasta to the boiling water and cook it for 2 to 3 fewer minutes than listed on the package.

While the rigatoni is cooking, transfer the cooked sweet potato, cauliflower, garlic and cashews to a blender. Rinse the colander and set it aside.

Add the water, lemon juice, coconut aminos, mustard, nutritional yeast, miso, onion powder, paprika, turmeric, salt, black pepper and tapioca flour to the blender. Blend the ingredients at high speed until they are completely smooth and creamy. Season the sauce with additional salt if desired.

Drain the pasta in the rinsed colander and set it aside. Pour the sauce into the saucepan and set it over low heat. Cook the sauce for 2 to 3 minutes, stirring it constantly, until it has slightly thickened. Add the pasta to the sauce and gently fold it into the sauce to coat it evenly. Pour the pasta into the prepared baking dish and sprinkle the top of the pasta with the cauliflower bread crumbs.

Bake the mac and cheese, uncovered, for 10 to 15 minutes, until the bread crumbs are toasted and the sauce is bubbly. Remove the mac and cheese from the oven and serve it right away.

## Crispy Cauliflower

1 medium head cauliflower

¾ cup (71 g) super-fine almond flour

1 tbsp (9 g) tapioca flour

⅔ cup (160 ml) water

½ tsp salt

⅓ cup (36 g) cauliflower bread crumbs or ⅓ cup (28 g) almond meal

## Teriyaki Sauce

½ cup (120 ml) coconut aminos, Bragg Liquid Aminos, soy sauce or tamari

¼ cup (48 g) coconut sugar

1 tbsp (14 g) minced fresh ginger

2 cloves garlic, minced

3 tbsp (45 ml) mirin

2 tbsp (30 ml) chili-garlic sauce

¼ tsp salt

1 tbsp (15 ml) unseasoned rice vinegar

2 tbsp (30 ml) water

1 tsp tapioca flour

# TASTY-AS-TAKEOUT TERIYAKI CAULIFLOWER BOWLS

### Yields 4 servings

*You dim sum and you lose sum, and this recipe is a total win! It truly is just as tasty as takeout and is proof that eating a clean plant-based diet doesn't mean you have to compromise on flavor or miss out on your favorite takeout dishes while enjoying the newest rom-com on the couch. Preparing a dish that traditionally is loaded with sodium, refined sugar, oil and artificial flavors with whole, pure ingredients means it's much better for you—and in this case, just as delicious! I love this recipe because the lightly breaded cauliflower pieces are perfectly tender and crisp, and the teriyaki is filled with familiar bold and delightful flavors. Say buh-bye to takeout. This recipe is sure to satisfy.*

To make the crispy cauliflower, preheat the oven to 400°F (204°C). Line a large baking sheet with parchment paper.

Cut the cauliflower into 1½-inch (4-cm) florets, removing any stems. Leave the florets on the cutting board while you prepare the batter: In a large bowl, combine the almond flour, tapioca flour, water and salt. Whisk the ingredients with a fork to thoroughly combine them. The consistency should be just slightly thinner than pancake batter.

Transfer the cauliflower florets to the bowl of batter and use the fork to gently toss the florets in the batter. Make sure they are evenly coated with batter. Sprinkle the florets with the cauliflower bread crumbs.

One at a time, remove the florets from the batter, letting any excess drip off. Place each floret on the prepared baking sheet, spacing the florets at least 1 inch (2.5 cm) apart. Bake the cauliflower for 25 to 30 minutes, until it is lightly golden and crispy. Rinse out the bowl, dry it and set it aside.

While the cauliflower is baking, make the teriyaki sauce. In a small saucepan over low heat, combine the coconut aminos, sugar, ginger, garlic, mirin, chili-garlic sauce, salt, vinegar, water and tapioca flour. Bring the sauce to a gentle simmer and cook it for 5 to 7 minutes, stirring it frequently, until it has thickened.

(continued)

### Accompaniments

1 large bunch broccolini

1 cup (155 g) shelled edamame

12 oz (336 g) heart of palm rice or rice of choice, cooked

1 tbsp (9 g) black sesame seeds, for garnish

To prepare the accompaniments, place the broccolini and edamame in a steamer basket sitting on a medium saucepan filled with water. Bring the water to a boil over high heat and steam the broccolini and edamame for 3 to 4 minutes, until they are tender and vibrantly green.

Remove the cauliflower from the oven and set it aside to cool for 3 to 5 minutes. Allowing the cauliflower to cool prevents steaming when you toss it with the sauce, which prevents mushiness and keeps it crispy. Transfer the crispy cauliflower to the rinsed and dried large bowl and pour the teriyaki sauce over the florets. Very gently toss the cauliflower to coat it in the teriyaki sauce.

To serve, divide the rice among four bowls and top each bowl of rice with the teriyaki cauliflower, broccolini and edamame. Garnish each serving with the sesame seeds.

## CRISPY CHIPOTLE JACKFRUIT TAQUITOS

### Yields 4 servings

### Taquito Filling

28 oz (784 g) canned young green jackfruit, drained and rinsed

Water, vegetable broth or avocado oil, as needed

½ small red onion, finely chopped

2 cloves garlic, minced

1 large carrot, shredded

3 tbsp (45 ml) water, divided and as needed

1 (7-oz [196-g]) can chipotle peppers in adobo sauce

1 (14-oz [392-g]) can pinto beans, drained, ¼ cup (60 ml) liquid reserved

½ tsp salt

½ tsp black pepper

½ tsp garlic powder

½ tsp paprika

2 tbsp (22 g) nutritional yeast

8 (6 or 8" [15- or 20-cm]) almond flour tortillas

If you haven't tried jackfruit before, this recipe is a fabulous introduction. A bit of fun trivia for you: The jackfruit is the largest tree fruit in the world, with each fruit reaching up to 100 pounds (45 kg). One could say its size is matched by its culinary greatness. Once ripe, the jackfruit is incredibly sweet, reminiscent of mango or pineapple. However, when harvested young (which is the variety we will use in this recipe), the flesh of the jackfruit has very little flavor and a fibrous texture similar to that of shredded chicken or pork, making it a profoundly versatile plant-based meat substitute. I adore this fun and flavorful recipe as a party appetizer, a main course at a tailgate or an easy weeknight dinner.

To make the taquito filling, preheat the oven to 400°F (204°C). Line a large baking sheet with parchment paper.

Place the jackfruit pieces on a clean kitchen towel. Wrap the jackfruit in the towel and squeeze out any excess moisture over the sink. Unwrap the towel and use your fingers to shred the jackfruit into thin, stringy pieces over a medium bowl. Coarsely chop the firmer pieces if needed.

Heat a large cast-iron skillet over medium heat. Add a small amount of water to coat the bottom of the skillet. Add the onion and garlic and sauté them for 2 minutes, until they are fragrant. Add the carrot and jackfruit to the skillet, and then add 1 tablespoon (15 ml) of water to deglaze the skillet if needed. Spread the ingredients out into an even layer and cook them for 5 to 7 minutes, stirring them only every 1 to 2 minutes to let the jackfruit get a bit crispy on each side.

While the jackfruit is cooking, place the chipotle peppers with the adobo sauce in a blender and puree the peppers, adding up to 2 tablespoons (30 ml) of water to thin the puree if needed.

When the edges of the jackfruit are beginning to brown, pour the chipotle pepper sauce into the skillet. Reduce the heat to low and stir to coat the jackfruit and veggies in the sauce. Remove the skillet from the heat and set it aside.

Put the pinto beans and their reserved liquid in a large bowl. Use a potato masher, flat-bottomed glass or fork to roughly mash the beans, leaving some chunkiness. Stir in the salt, black pepper, garlic powder, paprika and nutritional yeast.

(continued)

Refreshing Yogurt Sauce

1 cup (240 ml) plain unsweetened vegan Greek yogurt

2 tsp (4 g) lime zest

2 tbsp (30 ml) fresh lime juice

2 tsp (2 g) finely chopped fresh cilantro

⅛ tsp salt

⅛ tsp black pepper

For Serving

½ cup (35 g) shredded red cabbage

½ cup (75 g) cherry tomatoes, coarsely chopped

¼ cup (4 g) finely chopped fresh cilantro leaves

Prepare the taquitos by layering the bean mixture in a 1-inch (2.5-cm)-wide strip down the center of each tortilla. Top the bean mixture with the jackfruit-veggie mixture. Lay the filled tortilla on a flat surface and wrap it up tightly by rolling it away from you. Place each taquito on the prepared baking sheet, seam side down. Bake the taquitos for 15 to 18 minutes, until the exteriors of the tortillas are lightly golden and crispy.

While the taquitos are baking, prepare the refreshing yogurt sauce. In a medium jar, use a fork to whisk together the yogurt, lime zest, lime juice, cilantro, salt and black pepper. On its own, the sauce will taste mild, but it is a perfect complement to the spicy and savory taquitos.

Remove the taquitos from the oven. Drizzle the hot taquitos with the refreshing yogurt sauce, or serve the sauce on the side for dipping. Top the taquitos with the cabbage, tomatoes and cilantro and serve them immediately.

If you have leftovers, these taquitos can be stored in the fridge for up to 1 week. They can also be stored in an airtight container in the freezer for up to 6 months. To reheat the taquitos, place them on a baking sheet and bake them at 300°F (149°C) for 10 to 20 minutes, until they are heated through.

1 large or 2 small sweet potatoes, peeled and cubed (about 3 cups [402 g])

¾ cup (68 g) gluten-free oat flour

1 tbsp (9 g) tapioca flour

½ tsp salt

1 tbsp (11 g) nutritional yeast

Creamy Roasted Red Pepper Sauce

½ cup (73 g) raw cashews

¼ cup (60 ml) water

1 cup (149 g) coarsely chopped fire-roasted red bell peppers

¼ cup (44 g) nutritional yeast

Juice of ½ small lemon

1 clove garlic

1 tsp paprika

1 tbsp (15 ml) pure maple syrup

½ tsp salt, plus more as needed

½ tsp black pepper, plus more as needed

# SWEET POTATO GNOCCHI WITH CREAMY ROASTED RED PEPPER SAUCE

## Yields 4 servings

Gnocchi has to be one of the most comforting foods out there, and this gnocchi gets extra comfort points because it's made from tender, flavorful sweet potatoes. The texture is classic-gnocchi perfection, and the quick roasted red pepper sauce is the perfect balance of creamy, savory, spicy and sweet. The sauce is also stunningly vibrant, making for a beautiful dinner plate. Your guests will not believe this recipe is both gluten-free and vegan.

To make the gnocchi, place the sweet potatoes in a steamer basket and place the basket in a medium saucepan filled with 1 inch (2.5 cm) of water. Steam the sweet potatoes for 12 minutes, until they are fork-tender. Remove the sweet potatoes from the heat and set them aside to cool slightly.

Meanwhile, prepare the creamy roasted red pepper sauce. In a high-speed blender, combine the cashews, water, bell peppers, nutritional yeast, lemon juice, garlic, paprika, maple syrup, salt and black pepper. Blend the ingredients at high speed until they are completely smooth and creamy. Season the sauce with additional salt and black pepper if desired. Set the sauce aside.

When the sweet potato cubes are no longer steaming, transfer them to a medium bowl and use a potato masher to thoroughly mash the potatoes. Add the oat flour, tapioca flour, salt and nutritional yeast. Use a hand mixer, running at low speed, to mix the ingredients until a dough forms. Your dough should not be too wet or sticky, nor dry and crumbly. Add 1 tablespoon (6 g) of oat flour to overly wet dough or 1 tablespoon (15 ml) of water to overly dry dough. Roll the dough into a ball.

Divide the dough into 4 evenly sized balls and place them on a large cutting board. Use your hands to gently roll each ball into a rope that is roughly 8 inches (20 cm) long and 1 inch (2.5 cm) thick. Use a paring knife or butter knife to slice each dough rope into 1-inch (2.5-cm)-long gnocchi pieces.

Fill a medium saucepan two-thirds full with water and bring it to a boil over high heat. Cook the gnocchi in three or four batches: Use a slotted spoon to gently place some of the gnocchi into the boiling water. Boil the gnocchi for about 2 minutes, until they float to the surface. Use a slotted spoon to remove the gnocchi from the water and transfer them to a colander to let excess water drain away. Drain the cooking water from the saucepan.

Transfer the gnocchi back to the saucepan and add the creamy roasted red pepper sauce, tossing the gnocchi to coat them in the sauce.

(continued)

For Serving

6 cups (180 g) baby spinach,
roughly chopped

3–4 leaves fresh basil, for garnish

Black pepper, for garnish

To serve the gnocchi, add the spinach to the saucepan and gently fold it into the gnocchi. Cook the gnocchi for 2 to 3 minutes, stirring it occasionally, until the spinach has wilted. Transfer the gnocchi to a serving dish and top it with the basil and black pepper.

For a crispier version of the gnocchi, heat a large cast-iron skillet over low heat and add in a bit of avocado oil, vegetable broth or water to coat the skillet. Arrange the gnocchi in a single layer and cook undisturbed for 2 to 3 minutes. Pour in the red pepper sauce and gently toss with a spoon to coat. Stir in the chopped spinach and leave the skillet over low heat for 1 to 2 minutes until the spinach has wilted, stirring occasionally. Use a chef's knife to chiffonade your basil leaves. Serve the gnocchi hot topped with fresh basil and freshly cracked black pepper.

TIP: If you would like to switch it up, this gnocchi also pairs beautifully with steamed broccoli or broccolini.

### Two-Ingredient Crusts

1 cup (90 g) gluten-free oat flour, plus more as needed

¾ cup (180 ml) plain unsweetened vegan Greek yogurt

¼ tsp salt

### Sauce and Toppings

2 tbsp (32 g) tomato paste

⅓ cup (80 ml) tomato sauce

⅓ cup (80 ml) plain unsweetened vegan Greek yogurt

1 tbsp (15 ml) pure maple syrup

1 tbsp (8 g) berbere seasoning

1 cup (164 g) canned chickpeas, drained

¼ cup red onion, thinly sliced

½ medium avocado, thinly sliced

¼ cup (4 g) finely chopped fresh cilantro leaves

1 Persian cucumber, quartered and coarsely chopped

# BERBERE-SPICED CHICKPEA FLATBREADS WITH TWO-INGREDIENT CRUSTS

## Yields 2 servings

Flatbreads are pizza's younger, cooler, more interesting cousin, and these flatbreads take the coolness up a notch with their gluten-free crusts—which call for only two ingredients besides salt—and plant-based toppings. The berbere seasoning brings a spicy, warm and slightly sweet flavor to the tomato sauce, which is perfectly paired with the creamy tofu ricotta and avocado slices. This recipe makes a crowd-pleasing party appetizer or a fun Friday night dinner at home!

To make the two-ingredient crusts, preheat the oven to 400°F (204°C).

In a large bowl, use a fork to combine the flour, yogurt and salt. Roll the dough into a ball. If the dough feels too sticky, add up to 1 tablespoon (6 g) more of oat flour. Divide the dough into two balls, and then lightly flour a large piece of parchment paper.

Place one dough ball on the prepared parchment paper. Use your hands to gently flatten the dough into an oval or round disk. Sprinkle a little more flour on top of the dough and cover it with a second sheet of parchment paper. Use a rolling pin to roll the dough into a ⅛-inch (3-mm)-thick crust. Remove the top sheet of parchment paper and transfer the crust, still on the bottom piece of parchment paper, to a large baking sheet or pizza pan. Use a fork to pierce the crust all over. Repeat this process with the second ball of dough. Prebake the crusts for 10 minutes.

While the crusts are prebaking, prepare the sauce and toppings. In a small bowl, combine the tomato paste, tomato sauce, yogurt, maple syrup and berbere seasoning. Transfer ⅓ cup (80 ml) of the sauce to a small bowl and set it aside. Add the chickpeas to the remaining sauce and toss them to coat them in the sauce.

Once the crusts are prebaked, use a spoon to divide the remaining ⅓ cup (80 ml) of sauce between the two crusts, leaving a ½-inch (1.3-cm) border of crust exposed around the edge. Use the same spoon to remove the chickpeas from their sauce, letting any excess drip off of them, and divide them between the two crusts. Sprinkle each flatbread with the red onion. Bake the topped flatbreads for 10 minutes, until the onions are soft and the crusts are lightly golden.

(continued)

Tofu Ricotta

6 oz (168 g) extra firm tofu

1 tbsp (17 g) white miso

1 tbsp (11 g) nutritional yeast

¼ tsp salt

⅛ tsp black pepper

1 tbsp (15 ml) fresh lemon juice

1 tsp garlic powder

1 tsp pure maple syrup

While the flatbreads are baking, prepare the tofu ricotta. In a food processor, combine the tofu, miso, nutritional yeast, salt, black pepper, lemon juice, garlic powder and maple syrup. Process the ingredients for 15 to 30 seconds, until the mixture is smooth and creamy.

Remove the flatbreads from the oven and top each one with four 1-tablespoon (15-g) dollops of the ricotta. Return the flatbreads to the oven and broil them on low for 1 to 2 minutes, watching them carefully, until the ricotta is slightly golden.

Remove the flatbreads from the oven and top each of them with the avocado, cilantro and cucumber. Slice them and serve them immediately.

## Tofu "Shrimp"

14 oz (392 g) extra firm tofu, pressed (see Tip on page 32) and broken into 1" (2.5-cm) pieces

1 tbsp (9 g) tapioca flour

1 tsp nori flakes

¼ cup (23 g) gluten-free oat flour

¼ cup (60 ml) water

¼ tsp salt

¼ tsp black pepper

## Bang-Bang Sauce

¼ cup (60 ml) plain unsweetened coconut yogurt

2 tbsp (30 ml) chili-garlic sauce

1 tbsp (15 ml) pure maple syrup

1 tsp fresh lime juice

## Tacos

4 (6 or 8" [15- or 20-cm]) almond flour tortillas

1 tsp black sesame seeds

1 green onion, finely chopped

½ cup (28 g) finely chopped green leaf lettuce

½ large avocado, thinly sliced

¼ cup (18 g) finely chopped red cabbage

1 Persian cucumber, thinly sliced

1 large lime, sliced into wedges

# BANG-BANG BAJA "SHRIMP" TACOS

## Yields 2 servings

Without naming names, this recipe was inspired by a very popular appetizer at a very popular seafood restaurant chain, but of course, I had to make it vegan, gluten-free and much healthier. The traditional recipe is made with animal products, gluten, dairy and high levels of saturated fat and sugar, and it is also fried and covered in a sauce made from mayonnaise and sugar. This spec-taco-lar recipe is just the opposite. It's 100 percent plant-based, baked (instead of fried) and lightly coated in a sauce made from whole ingredients. If you prefer, the "shrimp" taco filling can also be enjoyed on its own as an appetizer.

To make the tofu "shrimp," preheat the oven to 375°F (191°C). Line a large baking sheet with parchment paper.

Place the tofu in a medium bowl. Sprinkle the tapioca flour and nori flakes over the tofu. Use a rubber spatula to gently stir the tofu to coat it in the flour and nori.

In a small bowl, use a fork to stir together the oat flour, water, salt and black pepper to form a batter.

Pour the tofu into the batter and use the rubber spatula to gently fold the tofu pieces into the batter and coat them well. Wipe out the medium bowl and set it aside.

Use the fork to carefully remove each piece of tofu from the batter, letting excess batter drip off before placing the tofu on the prepared baking sheet. Bake the tofu for 20 to 25 minutes, until it is golden and crispy.

While the tofu "shrimp" is baking, prepare the bang-bang sauce. In the medium bowl that held the tofu, whisk together the yogurt, chili-garlic sauce, maple syrup and lime juice. Set the sauce aside.

When the tofu "shrimp" has about 5 minutes of baking time left, begin preparing the tacos. Warm each tortilla in a dry medium skillet over medium heat for 15 to 30 seconds per side, until they are slightly golden. Set the tortillas aside.

Remove the tofu "shrimp" from the oven and let it cool for 3 minutes. Transfer the tofu to the bowl of bang-bang sauce and use a rubber spatula to gently stir the tofu into the sauce. Immediately sprinkle the coated tofu with the sesame seeds and green onion.

Assemble the tacos by layering the lettuce, avocado, cabbage and cucumber in each tortilla and topping the veggies with the tofu "shrimp." Squeeze the lime wedges over each taco right before serving.

Water, vegetable broth or avocado oil, as needed

1 small yellow onion, minced

4 cloves garlic, minced

8 oz (224 g) cremini mushrooms, finely chopped

1 large carrot, finely grated

¼ cup (60 ml) red wine vinegar

2 tbsp (8 g) Italian seasoning

½ tsp red pepper flakes

2 tbsp (22 g) nutritional yeast

1 tsp salt

½ tsp black pepper

3 tbsp (48 g) tomato paste

1¼ cups (300 ml) tomato sauce

1 (14-oz [392-g]) can diced tomatoes, undrained

1½ cups (360 ml) water

1 cup (192 g) red lentils

12 oz (336 g) chickpea or lentil rigatoni

2 tbsp (8 g) finely chopped fresh parsley, for serving

¼ cup (62 g) Tofu Ricotta (page 47), for serving

# GRAIN-FREE RIGATONI WITH LENTIL BOLOGNESE SAUCE

## Yields 4 servings

Meatless Bolognese that is just as delicious and hearty as the real deal but secretly packed full of veggies and plant protein: Impastable? Think again! This plant-powered sauce is filled with protein from the red lentils and is slowly simmered, giving the complex flavors plenty of time to get acquainted. This is a cozy and satisfying weeknight meal that you will be making again and again.

Heat a large cast-iron skillet over medium-high heat. Add a small amount of water to coat the bottom of the skillet. Add the onion and garlic and sauté them for 1 to 2 minutes, until they are fragrant. Add the mushrooms and carrot and sauté the mixture for 3 to 4 minutes, until the veggies are becoming tender and the mushrooms have reduced in size. Reduce the heat to medium-low and add the vinegar, then sauté the mixture for 2 minutes, until the majority of the liquid has evaporated.

Add the Italian seasoning, red pepper flakes, nutritional yeast, salt, black pepper and tomato paste, and then sauté the mixture for 30 seconds. Pour in the tomato sauce, diced tomatoes and their liquid, water and lentils. Stir to combine the ingredients and bring them to a boil. Reduce the heat to low and allow the sauce to come to a gentle simmer. Cook the sauce for 30 minutes, until it has thickened and has a rich, meaty texture.

While the sauce is cooking, fill a large saucepan two-thirds full with water and bring it to a boil over high heat. Add the rigatoni. I find that lentil- and chickpea-based pastas often require less cooking time than specified on the package, so check the pasta for doneness 2 to 3 minutes earlier than recommended.

Drain the rigatoni in a colander, reserving ½ cup (120 ml) of the pasta water. Transfer the pasta to the pan of sauce and gently fold the pasta into the sauce, adding the reserved pasta water a bit at a time, if needed, to thin the sauce slightly and add creaminess. Serve the pasta hot, topped with the parsley and tofu ricotta.

## Noodle Bowls

1 lb (454 g) extra firm tofu, pressed (see Tip on page 32) and cut into 1" (2.5-cm) cubes

2 tbsp (30 ml) coconut aminos, Bragg Liquid Aminos, soy sauce or tamari, divided

Water, vegetable broth or avocado oil, as needed

1 lb (454 g) cremini mushrooms, thinly sliced

12 oz (336 g) brown rice ramen noodles

8 cups (240 g) baby spinach

1 large English cucumber, coarsely chopped

1 large avocado, thinly sliced

½ cup (8 g) fresh cilantro leaves, coarsely chopped

½ medium jalapeño, thinly sliced

1 tbsp (9 g) white sesame seeds

1 large lime, quartered, for serving

## Hoisin Sauce

¼ cup (60 g) date paste, plus more as needed

2 tbsp (30 ml) coconut aminos, Bragg Liquid Aminos, soy sauce or tamari

2 tbsp (30 ml) unseasoned rice vinegar

1 tbsp (15 ml) chili-garlic sauce, plus more as needed

2 tbsp (32 g) creamy natural peanut butter

½ tsp garlic powder

¼ tsp ground cinnamon

¼ tsp ground cloves

¼ cup (60 ml) water

# UMAMI NOODLE BOWLS WITH HOISIN-GLAZED TOFU

### Yields 4 servings

This meal makes miso happy because it takes very little effort but majorly delivers in the flavor department. Plus, in my opinion, everything tastes better when you use chopsticks! These bowls perfectly balance clean, fresh ingredients with a bold, crispy hoisin tofu and tender brown rice ramen noodles. The result is full of umami flavor and is sure to shoyu how delicious vegan food can be!

To make the noodle bowls, preheat the oven to 400°F (204°C). Line a large baking sheet with parchment paper.

Place the tofu cubes in a medium bowl and drizzle the tofu with 1 tablespoon (15 ml) of the coconut aminos. Gently toss the tofu cubes with a rubber spatula to coat them. Transfer the tofu cubes to the prepared baking sheet and set the bowl aside. Bake the tofu for 25 minutes, flipping it halfway through the baking time.

While the tofu is baking, heat a large cast-iron skillet over medium-high heat. Add a small amount of water to coat the bottom of the skillet. Add the mushrooms and sauté them for 2 to 3 minutes, until they begin to soften and reduce in size. Drizzle the mushrooms with the remaining 1 tablespoon (15 ml) of coconut aminos and sauté them for 3 to 4 minutes more, until they are golden and crispy.

While the mushrooms are cooking, prepare the ramen noodles in a medium saucepan according to the package's instructions. Drain the noodles and set them aside. To the same saucepan, add 1 inch (2.5 cm) of water and the spinach. Cover the saucepan, set it over high heat and steam the spinach for 3 minutes, until it is wilted. Drain the spinach and return it to the saucepan, covering the saucepan to keep the spinach warm.

To make the hoisin sauce, in the medium bowl that contained the tofu, whisk together the date paste, coconut aminos, vinegar, chili-garlic sauce, peanut butter, garlic powder, cinnamon, cloves and water. Season the sauce, adjusting the spice level with additional chili-garlic sauce or the level of sweetness with additional date paste.

Remove the tofu from the oven and transfer it to the bowl of hoisin sauce. Toss the tofu to evenly coat it with the sauce.

Prepare the noodle bowls by dividing the ramen noodles among four bowls and topping the noodles with the steamed spinach, sautéed mushrooms and crispy tofu. Top the bowls with the cucumber, avocado, cilantro, jalapeño and sesame seeds. Squeeze a wedge of lime over each bowl and serve.

## Wraps

12 oz (336 g) extra firm tofu, pressed (see Tip on page 32)

8 large collard green leaves (see Tip)

1 large avocado, thinly sliced

1 medium yellow mango, thinly sliced

2 large carrots, peeled and julienned

1 large red bell pepper, thinly sliced

1 cup (89 g) finely chopped red cabbage

½ large English cucumber, thinly sliced

½ cup (8 g) fresh cilantro leaves, coarsely chopped

2 cups (110 g) coarsely chopped romaine lettuce

1 cup (225 g) heart of palm noodles, cooked and cooled

## Thai Peanut Sauce

⅓ cup (86 g) creamy natural peanut butter

¼ cup (60 ml) fresh lime juice, plus more as needed

2 tbsp (30 ml) unseasoned rice vinegar

2 tbsp (30 ml) chili-garlic sauce, plus more as needed

3 tbsp (45 ml) pure maple syrup, plus more as needed

1 tbsp (15 ml) coconut aminos

1–2 tbsp (15–30 ml) water (optional)

2 tbsp (18 g) roasted unsalted peanuts, finely chopped

TIP: Look for collard leaves that are larger than your face with few holes and tears.

# RAINBOW COLLARD WRAPS WITH CREAMY THAI PEANUT SAUCE

## Yields 4 servings

This is hands down one of the most beloved recipes from my blog, so I just couldn't write a cookbook without it. The peanut sauce is so good that you will be eating it by the spoonful, and the wraps are so vibrantly stunning that they instantly become the highlight of any table. Even the pickiest eaters can't help but be enamored. Full of crisp veggies, sweet mango, creamy avocado and protein-packed tofu, these wraps are all that and then some. The peanut sauce is also delightful on noodles, salads and quinoa bowls.

To prepare the wraps, preheat the oven to 400°F (204°C). Line a large baking sheet with parchment paper.

Cut the tofu into ½-inch (1.3-cm)–wide strips. Arrange the tofu strips on the prepared baking sheet. Bake the tofu for 25 minutes, flipping it halfway through the baking time. Remove the tofu from the oven and set it aside to cool.

Meanwhile, cut the broad stems off the base of each collard green leaf. Fill a large bowl with ice water. Bring a large, shallow pot of water to a boil over high heat. Submerge a collard green leaf in the boiling water for 15 to 20 seconds, until it turns a vibrant green and feels pliable. Use tongs to remove the leaf from the pot and immediately transfer it to the bowl of ice water. Remove the leaf from the ice bath, letting excess water drip off of it. Set the leaf aside to dry. Repeat this process with the remaining collard green leaves.

Lay each leaf, with its spine horizontal to you, on a clean, dry surface. In the middle of the leaf and right on its spine, create layers of ingredients in this order: avocado, mango, tofu, carrots, red bell pepper, cabbage, cucumber, cilantro, lettuce and noodles. Fold in the outer sides of the collard leaf first, followed by the edge closest to you, and then roll the leaf tightly away from you. Place the wrap on a serving tray seam side down. Repeat this process with each of the remaining collard leaves.

To make the Thai peanut sauce, combine the peanut butter, lime juice, vinegar, chili-garlic sauce, maple syrup and coconut aminos in a blender. Blend the ingredients until they are smooth and creamy. If desired, add the water, 1 tablespoon (15 ml) at a time, for a thinner sauce. If needed, adjust the flavor of the sauce by adding more lime juice, chili-garlic sauce and maple syrup. Top with the chopped peanuts.

Serve the wraps immediately or let them chill in the fridge for 30 minutes. Slice the wraps in half if desired, and serve them with the Thai peanut sauce on the side. These wraps can be stored in airtight containers in the refrigerator for up to 5 days.

# SUPERFOOD SOUPS AND SANDWICHES

Picture your typical soup and sandwich lunch, and then reimagine it as healthy, exciting and vegan. That's what this soup-er chapter is all about. I've included a soup for every season and every craving and sandwiches that are going to have even the meat eaters in your life begging for a bite. Some of these recipes are vegan to their core, while others are healthy vegan takes on some of your favorites that would traditionally contain meat or dairy.

If you're wondering how to choose from the options in this vibrant chapter and where you should start, one of my favorite recipes in this entire book is the Balsamic Beet Spread from the Rainbow Veggie Sandwich on page 72. Also, you should never live through a summer without the Cucumber-Melon Gazpacho with Pine Nut Pico on page 61.

I hope you enjoy many of these clean vegan soups and sandwiches as workday lunches, as nourishment packed on adventures and as memory-makers during gatherings with friends and family.

# CURRIED RED LENTIL COCONUT SOUP

## Yields 8 servings

*Boldly speaking, this is one of the best soups I've ever had. It's perfectly creamy, full of flavor, loaded with plant protein and incredibly versatile. It can hold its own as a solo dish but is delightful with a piece of warm gluten-free bread for dipping, served alongside brown rice for extra heartiness or served on top of greens like my Life-Changing Massaged Kale (page 80) for a fun and refreshing spin on soup and salad. As many soups and curries do, this tasty pot of goodness gets even better on day two, so curry up and get cooking!*

2 cups (384 g) red lentils

Water, vegetable broth or avocado oil, as needed

1 medium yellow onion, finely chopped

4 cloves garlic, minced

2 tbsp (28 g) minced fresh ginger

2 tbsp (32 g) tomato paste

1 tsp cumin seeds

1 tsp salt

2½ tbsp (15 g) curry powder

1 tsp garam masala

1 tsp ground coriander

1 tsp ground turmeric

1 tsp paprika

½ tsp cayenne, plus more as needed

1 (14-oz [392-g]) can diced tomatoes, with juices

1 (14-oz [420-ml]) can full-fat coconut milk

1 tbsp (15 ml) pure maple syrup, plus more as needed

1 tbsp (15 ml) coconut aminos, Bragg Liquid Aminos, soy sauce or tamari

Juice of 1 large lime, plus more as needed

2 cups (60 g) baby spinach, coarsely chopped

½ cup (120 ml) plain unsweetened coconut yogurt, for serving

¼ cup (4 g) fresh cilantro leaves, for serving

Fill a medium saucepan two-thirds full with water. Bring the water to a boil over high heat. Add the lentils, reduce heat to medium-low and simmer the lentils for 7 minutes.

While the lentils are cooking, place a large Dutch oven or pot over medium heat. Add a small amount of water to the Dutch oven to coat its bottom. Add the onion, garlic and ginger and sauté for 3 to 4 minutes, until they are fragrant and tender. Add a bit more water to deglaze the bottom of the Dutch oven.

Add the tomato paste, cumin seeds, salt, curry powder, garam masala, coriander, turmeric, paprika and cayenne. Cook the mixture for 15 seconds, stirring it frequently, until the spices become fragrant. Pour in the tomatoes and their juices, coconut milk, maple syrup, coconut aminos and lime juice. Bring the mixture to a gentle boil.

Drain the cooked lentils and add them to the Dutch oven. Gently boil the soup for 10 minutes. Stir in the spinach and stir the soup until the spinach has wilted. Season the soup with additional cayenne, lime juice or maple syrup if desired.

Serve the soup hot, topped with a dollop of the yogurt and a sprinkle of the cilantro.

## Gazpacho

Zest and juice of 1 large lemon

¼ cup (60 ml) white balsamic vinegar

⅓ cup (49 g) raw cashews

1 tsp salt, plus more as needed

½ tsp black pepper, plus more as needed

1 clove garlic, peeled

½ cup (46 g) fresh mint leaves

½ cup (12 g) fresh basil leaves

1 large avocado, pitted and peeled

3 large tomatillos, papery skins removed, quartered

2 cups (340 g) cubed honeydew melon

1 large English cucumber, quartered

1 large green bell pepper, stem and seeds removed, coarsely chopped

1 tbsp (15 ml) pure maple syrup (optional)

1 cup (240 ml) water (optional)

½ cup (120 ml) plain unsweetened coconut yogurt, for serving

## Pine Nut Pico

1 Persian cucumber, finely chopped

1 large tomatillo, papery skin removed, finely chopped

1 cup (170 g) finely chopped honeydew melon

⅓ cup (45 g) toasted pine nuts, coarsely chopped

¼ cup (12 g) finely chopped fresh chives

2 tbsp (6 g) finely chopped fresh basil

½ tsp salt

⅛ tsp black pepper

1 tbsp (15 ml) fresh lemon juice

½ cup (75 g) cherry tomatoes, finely chopped

# CUCUMBER–MELON GAZPACHO WITH PINE NUT PICO

### Yields 6 servings

Even if you think you don't like chilled soups, believe me—you're about to *love* chilled soups. This silky, refreshing soup is bursting with flavor and topped with a crisp and vibrant pine nut pico. The melon adds a subtle sweetness to complement the vegetables and herbs. Licking the bowl is not only appropriate, but encouraged. The best part of this recipe? You can make this soup in a matter of minutes—simply add the ingredients to a blender, blend them and enjoy!

To make the gazpacho, place the lemon zest and juice, vinegar, cashews, salt, black pepper, garlic, mint, basil, avocado, tomatillos, melon, English cucumber and bell pepper in a high-speed blender. Blend the ingredients at high speed for 60 to 90 seconds, until the mixture is smooth and creamy. Taste the gazpacho. Depending on the ripeness of your melon, you may choose to add the maple syrup if more sweetness is needed. Season the gazpacho with additional salt or black pepper if needed. If you like a thinner gazpacho, add up to 1 cup (240 ml) of water and blend the soup until the desired texture is achieved. Put the lid on the blender jar and place the gazpacho in the fridge to chill for at least 30 minutes, or preferably overnight.

While the gazpacho is chilling, prepare the pine nut pico. In a small bowl, use a fork to combine the Persian cucumber, tomatillo, melon, pine nuts, chives, basil, salt, black pepper, lemon juice and tomatoes. Cover the pico and place it in the fridge to chill for at least 30 minutes.

To serve, pour the gazpacho into four serving bowls. Add 2 tablespoons (30 ml) of the yogurt to each bowl and swirl it with a fork to disperse it into the soup. Top each serving with the pine nut pico and serve.

## Soup

20 oz (560 g) canned young green jackfruit, drained and rinsed

Water, vegetable broth or avocado oil, as needed

1 medium red onion, finely chopped

4 cloves garlic, minced

2 large poblano peppers, coarsely chopped

1½ tbsp (12 g) chili powder

1 tsp ground coriander

1 tsp paprika

2 tsp (4 g) ground cumin

2 tbsp (22 g) nutritional yeast

1 tsp salt, plus more as needed

1 tsp black pepper, plus more as needed

1 (8-oz [240-ml]) can tomato sauce

1 (14-oz [392-g]) can diced tomatoes, with juices

2 tbsp (32 g) tomato paste

1 (14-oz [420-ml]) can full-fat coconut milk

1 tbsp (15 ml) chili-garlic sauce, plus more as needed

1 (14-oz [392-g]) can black beans, drained

1 cup (136 g) frozen corn, thawed

Juice of 1 large lime, plus more as needed

½ cup (8 g) coarsely chopped fresh cilantro leaves

# CHICKEN TORTILLA SOUP, HOLD THE CHICKEN

## Yields 6 servings

That's right—no chickens were harmed in the making of this delicious chicken tortilla soup. That perfectly tender shredded "meat" comes from the wonderful jackfruit. This fabulous fruit is a great plant-based alternative when you're looking for the texture of shredded chicken. In this recipe, it takes on all the spicy flavors of this creamy southwestern soup and adds the perfect shredded-chicken texture. I adore this soup year-round and can't wait for you to try it. It is even meat eater approved!

Preheat the oven to 350°F (177°C). Line a large baking sheet with parchment paper.

To make the soup, place the jackfruit in the center of a clean kitchen towel. Wrap the jackfruit in the towel and use your hands to squeeze excess moisture from the jackfruit over the sink. Unwrap the towel and use your fingers to shred the jackfruit into small, stringy pieces, placing the pieces in a medium bowl as you go.

Heat a small amount of water in a large pot or Dutch oven over medium-low heat. Add the onion and garlic and sauté them for 2 minutes, until they are tender. Add the poblano peppers and jackfruit. Increase the heat to high and sauté the mixture for 2 to 3 minutes, until the poblano peppers are tender. Add additional water 1 tablespoon (15 ml) at a time to deglaze the pot if needed.

Add the chili powder, coriander, paprika, cumin, nutritional yeast, salt and black pepper. Cook the mixture for 30 seconds, stirring it frequently. Add the tomato sauce, diced tomatoes with their juices, tomato paste, coconut milk and chili-garlic sauce. Bring the mixture to a boil. Reduce the heat to medium and simmer the mixture for 15 minutes.

(continued)

### Crispy Tortilla Strips

4 (6 or 8" [15 or 20-cm]) almond flour soft tortillas, halved and sliced crosswise into strips

Avocado oil spray (optional)

### For Serving

1 large avocado, cubed

½ cup (120 ml) plain unsweetened vegan Greek yogurt

¼ cup (4 g) coarsely chopped fresh cilantro leaves

1 large lime, sliced into 6 wedges

Meanwhile, make the crispy tortilla strips. Spread the tortilla strips on the prepared baking sheet. Lightly spray the tortilla strips with the avocado oil (if using). Bake the tortilla strips for 10 to 12 minutes, until they are slightly golden and crispy.

Stir the beans, corn, lime juice and cilantro into the soup. Cook the soup for 5 minutes to heat the ingredients through. Season the soup with additional salt, black pepper, lime juice or chili-garlic sauce if needed.

Serve the soup hot topped with the avocado, yogurt, cilantro and tortilla strips, with the lime wedges on the side.

## Chili

Water, vegetable broth or avocado oil, as needed

1 medium red onion, diced

4 cloves garlic, minced

3 large ribs celery, finely chopped

3 medium carrots, finely chopped

8 oz (224 g) cremini mushrooms, halved and finely chopped

1 large red bell pepper, finely chopped

1 large orange bell pepper, finely chopped

1 cup (170 g) white quinoa

1½ tbsp (12 g) chili powder

2 tsp (5 g) paprika

2 tsp (4 g) ground cumin

1 tsp vegan Worcestershire powder

1 tsp salt

1 tsp black pepper

¼ cup (22 g) raw unsweetened cacao powder

1 (7-oz [196-g]) can chipotle peppers in adobo sauce, finely chopped, adobo sauce reserved

2 tbsp (30 ml) coconut aminos, Bragg Liquid Aminos, soy sauce or tamari

2 tbsp (30 ml) balsamic vinegar

1 (28-oz [794-g]) can diced tomatoes, with juices

# HEARTY THREE–BEAN QUINOA CHILI

## Yields 8 to 10 servings

This is the only chili recipe you need, and yes, it's vegan. Cue the mic drop. In all seriousness, this recipe dishes out the hearty meatiness of traditional chili, so even carnivores are guaranteed to be begging for more. The quinoa and beans are wonderful plant protein sources, with the quinoa providing every essential amino acid, and this recipe is also full of veggies, making it just as healthy as it is delicious. I love adding chipotle peppers in adobo to this recipe to provide some extra heat and a little smokiness, which is perfectly matched with a cool and creamy vegan yogurt.

To make the chili, heat a large Dutch oven or pot over medium heat. Add a small amount of water to the Dutch oven to coat its bottom. Add the onion, garlic, celery and carrots and sauté them for 4 to 5 minutes, stirring them occasionally and adding additional water to deglaze the Dutch oven as needed, until the celery and carrots soften slightly. Add the mushrooms, red bell pepper and orange bell pepper and sauté the veggies for 2 to 3 minutes, until the bell peppers soften slightly and the mushrooms release their juices.

If needed, add a bit more water to deglaze the Dutch oven, and then add the quinoa, chili powder, paprika, cumin, Worcestershire powder, salt, black pepper and cacao powder. Cook the mixture for 30 seconds, stirring it frequently, until the spices are fragrant. Add the chipotle peppers with the reserved adobo sauce, coconut aminos, vinegar, diced tomatoes with their juices, tomato paste and water. Bring the mixture to a boil, reduce the heat to medium-low and simmer the chili for 20 minutes, stirring it occasionally, until the chili thickens and the quinoa is soft.

(continued)

2 tbsp (32 g) tomato paste

3 cups (720 ml) water

1 (14-oz [392-g]) can dark red kidney beans, drained

1 (14-oz [392-g]) can light red kidney beans, drained

1 (14-oz [392-g]) can black beans, drained

2 tbsp (30 ml) pure maple syrup

Juice of 1 small lime

½ cup (8 g) coarsely chopped fresh cilantro leaves

1 cup (30 g) baby spinach, coarsely chopped

1 cup (149 g) cherry tomatoes, halved

### For Serving

1 cup (240 ml) plain unsweetened vegan Greek yogurt

1 small jalapeño, thinly sliced

¼ cup (4 g) coarsely chopped fresh cilantro leaves

Stir in the dark red kidney beans, light red kidney beans, black beans, maple syrup, lime juice, cilantro, spinach and cherry tomatoes. Simmer the chili for 2 to 3 minutes, stirring it frequently, until the spinach has wilted and the beans are heated through.

Serve the chili hot, topped with the yogurt, jalapeño and cilantro. This is a great chili to throw in the freezer, especially since it makes such a big batch, and its flavor gets even better the longer it sits. It can be stored in the freezer for up to 6 months.

Water, vegetable broth or avocado oil, as needed

1 large leek, green parts discarded, white parts finely chopped

4 cloves garlic, minced

1 small sweet potato, peeled and cut into ½" (1.3-cm) cubes

2 large carrots, peeled and diced

2 large ribs celery, finely chopped

1 large red bell pepper, diced

1 tsp dried parsley

1 tsp dried thyme

1 tsp dried oregano

1 tsp ground coriander

1½ tsp (9 g) salt, plus more as needed

½ tsp black pepper, plus more as needed

½ tsp red pepper flakes (optional)

1 tsp ground turmeric

1 tbsp (11 g) nutritional yeast

2 dried bay leaves

8 cups (1.9 L) water

2 (14-oz [392-g]) cans white beans, drained

10 oz (280 g) canned artichoke hearts, drained and finely chopped

1 small bunch lacinato kale, spines removed, finely chopped

1 tbsp (6 g) lemon zest

1 tbsp (15 ml) fresh lemon juice

½ cup (30 g) finely chopped fresh flat-leaf parsley

# MEDITERRANEAN WHITE BEAN VEGGIE SOUP

## Yields 8 servings

I love soup year-round, and this is definitely one for every season. The sweet potato makes it cozy and hearty enough for fall or winter, but the citrus and herbs mean it's always the right thyme for this recipe—even in spring and summer. Enjoy a bowl with a piece of crusty gluten-free bread to satisfy and delight.

Heat a large Dutch oven or pot over medium heat. Add a small amount of water to the Dutch oven to coat its bottom. Add the leek and garlic and sauté them for 1 minute, until they are fragrant. Add the sweet potato, carrots and celery and reduce the heat to medium-low, adding a bit more water to deglaze the bottom of the Dutch oven if needed. Cook the mixture for 4 to 5 minutes, stirring it every minute, until the sweet potato begins to soften. Add the bell pepper and sauté the mixture for 2 minutes, stirring it occasionally.

Add the dried parsley, thyme, oregano, coriander, salt, black pepper, red pepper flakes (if using), turmeric and nutritional yeast and stir the ingredients to combine them. Add the bay leaves. Pour in the water and bring the mixture to a boil over high heat. Reduce the heat to medium-low and simmer the mixture for 15 minutes. Stir in the beans, artichoke hearts, kale, lemon zest, lemon juice and fresh parsley. Simmer the soup for 2 to 3 minutes, until the kale is wilted and the beans are heated through. Taste the soup and season it with additional salt and black pepper if desired. Serve the soup hot.

## Soup

Avocado oil spray

1 large Pink Lady or Honeycrisp apple, cubed

1 small yellow onion, diced

3 cloves garlic

1½ lbs (681 g) carrots, peeled and sliced into 1" (2.5-cm)-thick pieces (about 12 medium carrots)

3 tbsp (45 ml) fresh lemon juice, divided

1 tsp avocado oil (optional)

2 tbsp (18 g) sumac

1 tsp salt, plus more as needed

1 tsp black pepper, plus more as needed

1 tsp dried oregano

½ tsp cayenne

1¾ cups (420 ml) water

1 (14-oz [420-ml]) can full-fat coconut milk

1" (2.5-cm) piece fresh ginger, peeled

1 tbsp (15 ml) tamari, coconut aminos or Bragg Liquid Aminos

1 tbsp (15 ml) pure maple syrup

1 tbsp (16 g) tomato paste

1 tbsp (15 ml) chili-garlic sauce

2 tbsp (30 ml) runny tahini

## Za'atar-Roasted Chickpeas

1 (14-oz [392-g]) can chickpeas, drained, rinsed and patted dry

1 tsp coconut aminos, Bragg Liquid Aminos, soy sauce or tamari

½ tsp garlic powder

½ tsp sumac

½ tsp dried oregano

1 tsp sesame seeds

½ tsp salt

½ tsp black pepper

# CREAMY SPICED CARROT SOUP WITH ZA'ATAR–ROASTED CHICKPEAS

## Yields 6 servings

Have you heard of a one-pot soup? Well, this is a no-pot soup! The ingredients are roasted and then blended for a silky soup that is ready in no time. This creamy Middle Eastern–inspired blend is just as bright and vibrant as it is spicy and earthy. The smooth texture meets your lips with a light burst of ginger and lemon and carries through to the finish with bold and warming depth from the sumac and tahini. Each bite of this creamy soup wouldn't be complete without the crunchy topping, chickpeas—so don't skip them!

---

Preheat the oven to 425°F (218°C). Line one large baking sheet with aluminum foil and another with parchment paper. Lightly coat the foil-lined baking sheet with the avocado oil spray.

To begin preparing the soup, combine the apple, onion, garlic and carrots in a large bowl. Drizzle them with 1 tablespoon (15 ml) of the lemon juice and the oil (if using). Toss the ingredients to combine them. Sprinkle the sumac, salt, black pepper, oregano and cayenne over the mixture and toss the ingredients to combine them. Spread the apple-veggie mixture on the foil-lined baking sheet. Set the bowl aside. Roast the apple-veggie mixture for 30 minutes, until the apple and carrot pieces are soft and their edges are golden.

To make the za'atar-roasted chickpeas, place the chickpeas in the bowl that contained the apple-veggie mixture. Drizzle the chickpeas with the coconut aminos. Add the garlic powder, sumac, oregano, sesame seeds, salt and black pepper and toss the chickpeas to evenly coat them in the seasonings. Spread the chickpeas on the parchment-lined baking sheet and roast them for 35 to 40 minutes, shaking the baking sheet to rotate the chickpeas halfway through the roasting time, until they are crispy. Begin checking the chickpeas for doneness frequently during the last 10 minutes of roasting time.

Transfer the roasted apple-veggie mixture to a high-speed blender. Add the remaining 2 tablespoons (30 ml) of lemon juice, water, coconut milk, ginger, tamari, maple syrup, tomato paste, chili-garlic sauce and tahini. Blend the mixture for 60 to 90 seconds, until the soup is completely smooth. Alternatively, you can transfer all of the ingredients to a large mixing bowl and blend them using an immersion blender.

Taste the soup and add more salt and black pepper if desired. Pour the soup straight from the blender into six serving bowls. Remove the chickpeas from the oven and sprinkle them on top of each serving of soup.

## Balsamic Beet Spread
### (Makes 1 cup [227 g])

⅔ cup (91 g) cubed raw beets (about 1 medium beet)

⅔ cup (97 g) raw cashews

2 tbsp (30 ml) balsamic vinegar

2 tbsp (30 ml) water

¼ tsp salt

### Sandwiches

8 slices gluten-free vegan bread, lightly toasted (see Tip)

1 cup (70 g) finely shredded red cabbage

8 large slices jarred fire-roasted red bell peppers, drained and patted dry

¼ cup (29 g) Quick Pickled Onions (page 18)

2 medium heirloom yellow tomatoes, thinly sliced into 8 slices

1 cup (33 g) alfalfa sprouts

1 cup (25 g) microgreens

# RAINBOW VEGGIE SANDWICH WITH BALSAMIC BEET SPREAD

## Yields 4 servings

If I had to pick one recipe that I am most excited to share in this book and can't live without, it would have to be this un-beet-able balsamic beet spread that truly makes this sandwich. It is perfectly sweet, perfectly creamy, bursting with flavor and the color is to die for. On this sandwich, the spread unites the flavors of the crisp, fresh veggies, but it is amazing on just about anything—crackers, jicama sticks, toast, tofu, pasta and salad; you name it!

To make the balsamic beet spread, place the beets, cashews, vinegar, water and salt in a high-speed blender. Blend the ingredients at high speed for 30 to 60 seconds, until the mixture is completely smooth and creamy. If you do not have a high-speed blender, you will need to boil the cashews for 10 minutes and allow them to cool prior to making the spread. At this point, you can use the spread immediately or chill it for an hour or two, as the flavors get better over time.

To assemble a sandwich in true rainbow fashion, layer the ingredients between two slices of bread in this order: cabbage, bell peppers, balsamic beet spread, Quick Pickled Onions, tomatoes, alfalfa sprouts and microgreens. Repeat this process with the remaining ingredients and serve the sandwiches immediately.

Leftover beet spread can be enjoyed for 7 to 10 days when stored in an airtight container in the fridge.

TIP: If you love making sandwiches with homemade bread, check out my Get Up and Go Super Seed Bread on page 131.

## Balsamic Fig Jam
### (Makes 1½ Cups [480 g])

1 cup (149 g) dried golden California figs, stems removed, finely chopped

1½ cups (360 ml) water

¼ cup (60 ml) fresh lemon juice

2 tbsp (30 ml) pure maple syrup

⅛ tsp salt

1 tbsp (10 g) chia seeds

2 tbsp (30 ml) balsamic vinegar

## Cauliflower-Cashew Mozzarella
### (Makes 2 Cups [480 ml])

2 cups (200 g) fresh or frozen cauliflower florets

½ cup (73 g) raw cashews

1 cup (240 ml) water

2 tbsp (22 g) nutritional yeast

1 tbsp (17 g) white miso

½ tsp salt

½ tsp Dijon mustard

1 tbsp (15 ml) fresh lemon juice

1 tsp apple cider vinegar

5 tbsp (40 g) arrowroot powder

## For the Grilled Cheese

Avocado oil spray (optional)

12 slices gluten-free vegan bread

1 cup (20 g) baby arugula

# FIG JAM AND MOZZARELLA GRILLED CHEESE

## Yields 6 servings

If a genie offered you one wish and you asked him to turn cauliflower into cheese, even he might laugh in your face. But your wish is my command! This vegan mozzarella is a dream come true: It's cheesy, stretchy, salty— and yes, it melts! Plus, it's made from wholesome ingredients like cashews and cauliflower. It may sound too good to be true, but it's the real deal and it is the perfect plant-based cheese substitute for this sandwich featuring a sweet fig jam and peppery arugula. Make the cheese and jam in advance for easy-to-assemble grilled cheeses that will be ready in just a few minutes after a long day at work.

To make the balsamic fig jam, combine the figs, water, lemon juice, maple syrup and salt in a small saucepan. Bring the mixture to a boil over high heat. Reduce the heat to low and simmer the mixture for 20 minutes, stirring it occasionally. Let the fig mixture cool slightly, and then transfer it to a high-speed blender. Add the chia seeds and balsamic vinegar. Pulse the blender until the balsamic fig jam reaches your desired consistency. Transfer the jam to a medium bowl and set it aside. Thoroughly clean the blender.

To make the cauliflower-cashew mozzarella, fill a medium saucepan two-thirds full with water and bring it to a boil over high heat. Add the cauliflower and cashews to the water, reduce the heat to medium and boil the cauliflower and cashews gently for 15 minutes. Drain the cauliflower and cashews in a colander, and then transfer them to the high-speed blender. Add the water, nutritional yeast, miso, salt, mustard, lemon juice, apple cider vinegar and arrowroot powder. Blend the ingredients at high speed for 1 minute, until no chunks remain. Pour the sauce into the saucepan and cook the mozzarella for 5 to 7 minutes over medium-high heat, stirring it constantly, until it thickens. Set the mozzarella aside.

Preheat a large cast-iron skillet over low heat, and then spray it lightly with the avocado oil spray (if using). Prepare a sandwich by spreading the mozzarella on one slice of the bread and spreading the balsamic fig jam on another slice of bread. Place the mozzarella-covered slice in the skillet with the mozzarella facing upward. Cover the skillet with its lid and let the bread toast for 2 to 3 minutes. Uncover the skillet and place a small handful of the arugula on the mozzarella. Top the arugula with the jam-covered slice of bread. Cook the sandwich, flipping it every 15 to 30 seconds, until your desired level of browning is achieved. Repeat this process with the remaining ingredients and serve the sandwiches immediately.

Leftover fig jam can be stored for up to a month in an airtight container in the fridge and is wonderful on toasted bread, like my Get Up and Go Super Seed Bread (page 131). Leftover mozzarella can be stored for up to 5 days in an airtight container in the fridge.

## "Tuna" Salad

1 (14-oz [392-g]) can chickpeas, drained

¼ cup (60 ml) runny tahini

2 tbsp (30 ml) plain unsweetened vegan yogurt

2 tsp (10 ml) Dijon mustard

Juice of ½ large lemon

1 tsp pure maple syrup

1 tbsp (11 g) nutritional yeast

¼ tsp salt, plus more as needed

⅛ tsp cayenne (optional)

¼ tsp black pepper, plus more as needed

1 tsp kelp granules

1 medium rib celery, finely chopped

¼ cup (31 g) finely chopped Honeycrisp, Gala or Pink Lady apple

2 tbsp (18 g) capers, coarsely chopped

¼ cup (36 g) finely chopped cornichons

¼ cup (25 g) sliced almonds, coarsely chopped

## For Serving

8 slices gluten-free vegan bread (see Tip)

8 leaves butter lettuce or romaine lettuce

1 large tomato, thinly sliced

½ cup (17 g) alfalfa sprouts

# NO TUNA TO SEA HERE SANDWICH

## Yields 4 servings

Unlike traditional tuna salad, no fish were harmed in the making of this familiarly delicious sandwich, so you can feel great about diving right in. With no shortage of flavor or plant protein, this creamy and tangy sandwich will delight your taste buds and satisfy any tuna salad cravings without doing any harm to our oceans.

To make the "tuna" sandwich filling, place the chickpeas in a medium bowl and use a potato masher or fork to roughly mash them—about half of the chickpeas should be mashed and half should be chunky. Add the tahini, yogurt, mustard, lemon juice, maple syrup, nutritional yeast, salt, cayenne (if using), black pepper and kelp granules. Use a fork to mix the ingredients together well. Add the celery, apple, capers, cornichons and almonds and stir the ingredients together until they are thoroughly combined. Taste the "tuna" salad and add more salt and black pepper if desired. Place the "tuna" salad in the fridge to chill for 30 minutes or overnight.

To prepare a sandwich, layer a slice of bread with a leaf of lettuce, "tuna" salad, tomato, alfalfa sprouts, another leaf of lettuce and additional alfalfa sprouts. Repeat this process with the remaining ingredients, and then serve the sandwiches.

TIP: This sandwich is fantastic on my Get Up and Go Super Seed Bread (page 131).

# GLOWING GREENS

When people hear the word *salad*, they automatically think of the word *healthy*. But truthfully, many of the salads out there are full of processed high-calorie ingredients and topped with dressings that are loaded with unhealthy saturated fats. This instantly turns your healthy bowl into just the opposite. But romaine calm—after reading this chapter you will see how salads can be absolutely delicious when made with real, whole ingredients. I am committed to the be-leaf that salads should always be healthy but never boring, and this chapter delivers a collection of my favorite salad recipes that are anything but bland! They're full of unique flavors, a variety of textures and hearty ingredients, meaning that many of these salads can be an entire meal all on their own.

This chapter includes salads that go way beyond your basic greens, and it kicks off with an explanation of massaged kale. If there is one thing you should take away from this book, it should be massaged kale. Massaging your kale will change your life—you'll believe me once you try it. So begin your salad adventure with Life-Changing Massaged Kale (page 80), and then flip to page 96 for my favorite salad recipe in the chapter: Moroccan Carrot Salad with Citrus-Turmeric Dressing, which is sure to delight everyone at your table.

1 large bunch lacinato kale

Juice of 1 medium lemon

½ tsp cold-pressed olive oil

⅛ tsp salt

⅛ tsp black pepper

# LIFE-CHANGING MASSAGED KALE

## Yields 4 servings

Would you believe me if I said I eat massaged kale alongside almost every single meal? If that sounds a little bizarre, or if you think you don't like kale in general, trust me when I say you're about to be craving kale in no time. This technique has turned the biggest kale haters into die-hard kale lovers with just one bite and has my husband constantly asking for more kale. Do I have your attention now?

By drizzling the kale with fresh lemon juice and a touch of cold-pressed oil and massaging the leaves with your hands until they are tender, the kale is softened and the bitter taste that typically gives kale a bad rap is eliminated. We're all a little less bitter after a massage, right? From there, you can enjoy kale on its own, add a little salt and pepper or top it with any dressing of your choice.

Almost every single recipe in this book pairs perfectly with massaged kale, and filling half of your plate with greens—specifically kale—as often as possible is an easy way to increase your consumption of veggies and nutrients. I love adding a bed of massaged kale to a bowl and topping it with anything from pasta, to curry, to chili, to crumbled veggie burgers, to taco "meat" or anything else you can think of.

Massaged kale is also a great way to fill up faster on low-calorie but nutrient-dense veggies. When it comes to caloric density, greens are extremely low-calorie but also very filling because they're full of fiber. One last thing I love about kale is that after being massaged, it will hold up perfectly in the fridge for several days. That means you can massage a big batch of kale on Sunday and have healthy, delicious, flavorful greens ready to add to any meal all week long!

Loosely grab each leaf of kale by the base and form a circle around it with your thumb and pointer finger. Using your other hand, pull the kale through the hole created by your fingers to remove the leafy greens from the rigid spine. Repeat this process with the remaining leaves.

Place the kale leaves in one compact bundle on a clean cutting board and use a large chef's knife to finely chop the kale, which will help the kale become even more tender. Transfer the chopped kale to a salad spinner or bowl and rinse it well, and then spin or drain the kale to dry it. Add the lemon juice, oil, salt and black pepper to the kale.

Using clean hands, massage the kale between your fingers for 15 to 30 seconds, until you feel it become more tender. You will be able to feel a difference, but you will also see a difference. Once the kale is massaged, it will have decreased in volume by about one-third. Serve the massaged kale as is, use it as a bed of greens beneath any main dish or top it with the dressing of your choice.

## ROASTED RED PEPPER CHICKPEA SALAD WITH RED WINE VINAIGRETTE

### Yields 6 servings

This is one of those salads that I could eat every single day and never tire of. The flavor is sweet and tangy, the chickpeas provide a hearty and filling protein base and the little pops of both fresh and roasted bell peppers are a delight. This salad is well rounded with some kick from the red onion and freshness of the parsley, making it the perfect side to accompany any meal. Traditional vinaigrettes are typically made with oil, but this recipe is totally oil-free, using aquafaba as an emulsifier and flavorless thickener—it is the perfect way to keep aquafaba from going to waste, since you are already utilizing chickpeas as an ingredient! This salad has stolen the show at numerous summer barbecues and is a recipe I am constantly requested to share with friends and family. It is best made the day before and takes only a few minutes to prepare.

### Salad

2 (14-oz [392-g]) cans chickpeas, drained, aquafaba reserved

1 (16-oz [454-g]) jar fire-roasted red bell peppers, drained and finely chopped

2 large green bell peppers, finely chopped

½ medium red onion, finely chopped

½ cup (30 g) finely chopped flat-leaf parsley

### Red Wine Vinaigrette

¼ cup (60 ml) red wine vinegar

3 tbsp (45 ml) reserved aquafaba

2 tbsp (30 ml) pure maple syrup, plus more as needed

½ tsp Dijon mustard

Juice of ½ large lemon

½ tsp salt, plus more as needed

½ tsp black pepper, plus more as needed

½ tsp garlic powder

To make the salad, place the chickpeas, red bell peppers, green bell peppers, onion and parsley in a medium glass bowl that has a lid. Using a large spoon, toss the ingredients to combine them.

To make the red wine vinaigrette, combine the vinegar, aquafaba, maple syrup, mustard, lemon juice, salt, black pepper and garlic powder in a blender. Blend the ingredients for 30 seconds, until the dressing is emulsified. Taste the vinaigrette and add more maple syrup, salt or black pepper if desired. Pour the dressing over the salad and use the large spoon to toss the salad with the dressing.

Cover the bowl with its lid and place the salad in the fridge to chill for at least 1 hour, or preferably overnight. Serve this salad cold on its own, alongside any main course, on a bed of greens like my Life-Changing Massaged Kale (page 80) or with rice or quinoa for a more filling dish.

## Salad

3 cups (255 g) broccoli florets, finely chopped

2 cups (310 g) shelled edamame

1 large red bell pepper, finely chopped

¼ cup (40 g) finely chopped red onion

¾ cup (110 g) roasted unsalted cashews, coarsely chopped

1 cup (113 g) coarsely chopped fresh snow peas

1 cup (16 g) finely chopped fresh cilantro leaves, plus more as needed

2 small, firm yellow mangoes, cubed

2 tbsp (18 g) black sesame seeds, plus more as needed

1 cup (185 g) quinoa, cooked and cooled completely

## Creamy Orange Dressing

⅓ cup (80 ml) fresh or refrigerated orange juice

2 tbsp (30 ml) unseasoned rice vinegar

Zest of 1 large lime

Juice of 1 large lime, plus more as needed

2 tbsp (30 ml) pure maple syrup, plus more as needed

2 tbsp (30 ml) coconut aminos, Bragg Liquid Aminos, soy sauce or tamari

1" (2.5-cm) piece fresh ginger, peeled

¼ cup (65 g) creamy natural cashew butter, almond butter or tahini

Salt, as needed

Black pepper, as needed

# CRUNCHY BROCCOLI-QUINOA SALAD WITH CREAMY ORANGE DRESSING

### Yields 6 servings

This tasty broccoli-quinoa salad is quick and easy to make and hearty enough to be a meal all on its own! The quinoa, edamame and cashews provide an abundance of plant protein, while the fresh veggies are rich in fiber and nutrients. The creamy orange dressing brings all of the ingredients together with an Asian-inspired flair and a subtle sweetness that means your loved ones will likely cashew going back for seconds.

To make the salad, combine the broccoli, edamame, bell pepper, onion, cashews, snow peas, cilantro, mangoes and sesame seeds in a large bowl. Use a large wooden spoon to gently mix the ingredients together. Add the quinoa to the bowl and use the wooden spoon to fold it into the other ingredients.

To make the dressing, combine the orange juice, vinegar, lime zest, lime juice, maple syrup, coconut aminos, ginger, cashew butter, salt and black pepper in a blender. Blend the ingredients for 30 seconds, until they are fully combined. Taste the dressing and season it with additional salt and black pepper. Adjust the sweetness with additional maple syrup or the tanginess with additional lime juice if desired.

Pour the dressing over the salad immediately prior to serving it and toss the salad to combine it with the dressing. Sprinkle the salad with additional sesame seeds and cilantro if desired.

## Salad

½ cup (68 g) raw hazelnuts

1 small bunch lacinato kale, stems removed, finely chopped

Juice of 1 small lemon

½ tsp cold-pressed olive oil

1½ cups (300 g) red rice, cooked and chilled

⅓ cup (53 g) unsweetened dried Bing cherries, coarsely chopped

⅓ cup (41 g) roasted salted pistachios, coarsely chopped

½ cup (46 g) finely chopped fresh mint leaves

½ cup (30 g) finely chopped fresh parsley

1 large shallot, finely chopped

Salt (optional)

Black pepper (optional)

## Balsamic-Lime Dressing

Zest of 2 large limes

Juice of 2 large limes

2 tbsp (30 ml) balsamic vinegar

1 tsp pure maple syrup

½ tsp salt, plus more

½ tsp black pepper

# HERBED RED RICE HAZELNUT SALAD

## Yields 6 servings

Rice in salad, especially red rice, is a wonderful thing. This variety of grain is incredibly rich in iron and vitamin B6 and has a deliciously warm, earthy and nutty flavor. The texture of the rice pairs perfectly with the lemony massaged kale, and the salad comes together with a mixture of sweet hazelnuts, tart cherries, fresh herbs and a balsamic-lime dressing. Enjoy this salad on its own or top it with roasted veggies, beans or tofu.

To make the salad, preheat the oven to 325°F (163°C). Line a small baking sheet with parchment paper. Spread the hazelnuts on the prepared baking sheet. Roast the hazelnuts for 10 to 12 minutes, shaking the baking sheet occasionally and checking frequently for doneness in the final 5 minutes to make sure they do not scorch. Remove the roasted hazelnuts from the oven and set them aside to cool for 5 minutes. Transfer them to a cutting board and chop them coarsely with a large knife.

In a large bowl, combine the kale, lemon juice and oil and massage the kale according to the instructions on page 80. Add the rice and hazelnuts to the kale, and then add the cherries, pistachios, mint, parsley and shallot. Use salad servers to mix the ingredients together. Set the salad aside.

To make the balsamic-lime dressing, use a fork to whisk together the lime zest, lime juice, vinegar, maple syrup, salt and black pepper.

Pour the dressing over the salad and use the salad servers to toss the salad with the dressing. Taste the salad and season it with the salt (if using) and black pepper (if using). Serve the salad chilled or at room temperature.

## Salad

1 large bunch lacinato kale, stems removed, finely chopped

Juice of 1 large lemon

½ tsp cold-pressed olive oil

2 cups (332 g) thinly sliced strawberries

1 large avocado, thinly sliced

2 Persian cucumbers, thinly sliced

½ cup (56 g) pecans, toasted and coarsely chopped

## Strawberry-Chia Vinaigrette

½ cup (83 g) quartered strawberries

1 soft, pitted Medjool date

¼ cup (60 ml) apple cider vinegar

Juice of 1 large lemon

1 tbsp (10 g) chia seeds

½ tsp salt

½ tsp black pepper

¼–½ cup (60 to 120 ml) water (see Tip)

# SUMMER SALAD WITH CREAMY STRAWBERRY–CHIA VINAIGRETTE

### Yields 4 servings

The second fresh strawberries become perfectly ripe in late spring or early summer, I immediately start making this salad on repeat. Few things go better together than strawberries, avocado and cucumber, and this refreshing, crisp salad combines all three! The homemade vinaigrette relies on blended chia seeds for a thick and creamy texture that delicately coats the berries and greens. To make this salad a more filling meal, add 1 cup (185 g) of cooked quinoa before serving.

To make the salad, combine the kale, lemon juice and oil in a large bowl. Massage the kale according to the instructions on page 80. Add the strawberries, avocado, cucumbers and pecans to the kale and toss the ingredients to combine them.

To make the strawberry-chia vinaigrette, combine the strawberries, date, vinegar, lemon juice, chia seeds, salt, black pepper and water in a blender. Blend the ingredients until they are smooth and emulsified.

Pour the vinaigrette over the salad just prior to serving it and use salad servers to toss the salad to coat it with the dressing. Serve the salad immediately.

TIP: For a thicker dressing, use ¼ cup (60 ml) of water. The dressing will thicken a bit as the chia seeds continue to absorb the liquid, so if you prefer a thinner dressing, use up to ½ cup (120 ml) of water.

## Salad

3 cups (165 g) dandelion greens or baby arugula, coarsely chopped

1 cup (130 g) finely chopped jicama

1 cup (70 g) finely shredded red cabbage

¼ cup (29 g) thinly sliced red onion

1 large avocado, thinly sliced

1 large orange, peeled and sliced into bite-sized pieces

1 large grapefruit, peeled and sliced into bite-sized pieces

¼ cup (34 g) pine nuts, toasted

## Super Greens Cilantro Dressing

Juice of 1 medium lemon

¼ cup (28 g) orange segments

¼ cup (60 ml) plain unsweetened coconut yogurt

¾ cup (12 g) tightly packed fresh cilantro

¼ cup (23 g) fresh mint leaves

1 clove garlic, peeled

½ tsp salt, plus more as needed

½ tsp black pepper, plus more as needed

1 tbsp (15 ml) pure maple syrup

1" (2.5-cm) piece fresh ginger, peeled

⅓ cup (80 ml) water

# JICAMA AND CITRUS SALAD WITH SUPER GREENS CILANTRO DRESSING

## Yields 4 servings

In my opinion, jicama has to be one of the most underrated vegetables around. It is perfectly crisp and crunchy, and its slightly sweet but overall neutral flavor pairs well with just about anything! In this vibrant bowl, it meets peppery and tender dandelion greens, sweet red cabbage, juicy orange, tart grapefruit and creamy avocado for a match that was truly made in heaven. All of these ingredients are tossed with a creamy super greens dressing that is bursting with ginger, citrus and herbs. This salad was meant for summer, and I can't wait for it to be on your table again and again all season long.

To make the salad, combine the dandelion greens, jicama, cabbage and onion in a large bowl. Use salad servers to toss the ingredients together. Add the avocado, orange, grapefruit and pine nuts and gently fold them into the mixture. Set the salad aside.

To make the super greens cilantro dressing, in a blender, combine the lemon juice, orange segments, yogurt, cilantro, mint, garlic, salt, black pepper, maple syrup, ginger and water. Blend the ingredients until they are smooth and creamy. Taste the dressing and add more salt and black pepper if desired.

Drizzle the dressing over the salad immediately prior to serving it and toss the salad to coat it with the dressing.

## Salad

Avocado oil spray

4 cups (680 g) peeled and cubed butternut squash

1 tbsp (15 ml) pure maple syrup

½ tsp salt

½ tsp black pepper

½ cup (96 g) black lentils

1 large bunch lacinato kale, stems removed, finely chopped

Juice of 1 large lemon

½ tsp cold-pressed olive oil

¼ cup (35 g) roasted unsalted pumpkin seeds

¼ cup (23 g) fresh mint leaves, finely chopped

¼ cup (15 g) finely chopped fresh parsley

1 cup (148 g) fresh blueberries

¼ cup (25 g) toasted walnuts, coarsely chopped

## Tangy Tahini Vinaigrette

¼ cup (60 ml) red wine vinegar

Juice of 1 large lemon

1 tbsp (15 ml) tahini

½ tsp sumac

½ tsp dried parsley

½ tsp garlic powder

1 tsp sesame seeds

1 tbsp (15 ml) pure maple syrup, plus more as needed

1 tsp Dijon mustard

¼ tsp salt, plus more as needed

½ tsp black pepper, plus more as needed

# BLACK LENTIL AND ROASTED SQUASH SALAD WITH TANGY TAHINI VINAIGRETTE

## Yields 4 servings

Black lentils are my favorite variety of lentils. They're tiny, full of nutty flavor, rich with plant protein and minerals and—best of all—their firm texture makes them ideal for salads! They add a delightful crunch and hold their shape, unlike other varieties of lentils. I love them combined with the roasted butternut squash and the brightness of the blueberries and herbs. These diverse ingredients are married together with a creamy tahini dressing full of vibrant lemon flavor!

To make the salad, preheat the oven to 400°F (204°C). Line a large baking sheet with parchment paper. Lightly spray the parchment paper with the avocado oil spray.

Place the butternut squash in a large bowl and drizzle the cubes with the maple syrup, and then season them with the salt and black pepper. Use a rubber spatula or large spoon to gently toss the squash to coat each cube. Spread the butternut squash cubes on the prepared baking sheet. Roast the squash for 30 to 35 minutes, until the cubes are golden and crispy. Remove the squash from the oven and let it cool for 5 minutes.

While the squash is roasting, fill a medium saucepan two-thirds full with water and bring it to a boil over high heat. Add the lentils, reduce the heat to medium-low and simmer the lentils for 12 to 13 minutes, until they are tender but not mushy. Drain the lentils and set them aside.

In a large bowl, combine the kale, lemon juice and olive oil. Massage the kale according to the instructions on page 80. Add the lentils, pumpkin seeds, mint, parsley, blueberries and walnuts to the kale and toss to combine the ingredients.

To make the tangy tahini vinaigrette, place the vinegar, lemon juice, tahini, sumac, parsley, garlic powder, sesame seeds, maple syrup, mustard, salt and black pepper in a blender. Blend the ingredients for 30 seconds, until they are smooth, creamy and emulsified. Season the dressing to taste, adjusting the sweetness with maple syrup or adding more salt and black pepper if desired.

Pour the dressing over the salad and toss to evenly coat it. Transfer the salad to serving bowls and top each serving with the roasted butternut squash.

## Salad

3 medium beets, tops and bottoms removed, peeled if desired

¾ cup (75 g) walnuts

2 tbsp (30 ml) pure maple syrup

⅛ tsp salt

¼ tsp ground cinnamon

1 batch Tofu Ricotta (page 47), chilled

1 cup (25 g) microgreens

10 fresh mint leaves, finely chopped

1 large Asian pear, cut into 1" (2.5-cm) cubes

Arils from 1 small pomegranate

## Balsamic Vinaigrette

¼ cup (60 ml) balsamic vinegar

1 tsp runny tahini

2 tsp (10 ml) Dijon mustard

1 tbsp (15 ml) pure maple syrup

Juice of 1 medium lemon

¼ tsp salt

¼ tsp black pepper

# BEET SALAD WITH TOFU RICOTTA, CANDIED WALNUTS AND BALSAMIC VINAIGRETTE

### Yields 4 servings

One of my mom's favorite stories to tell about me from my childhood was a time when I was no older than five and we were in a grocery store shopping in the produce department. I looked up at her with puppy dog eyes, clasped my hands together in a pleading gesture and said, "Mom, I beg you for beets!" Every other parent within earshot looked over in complete shock and awe. Needless to say, my love of beets runs deep. They were my absolute favorite food when I was a child, and I still adore them as an adult. Beets are easy to love, especially in this salad, and they're a great thing to love because of their wonderful nutrient profile. In this recipe, they are cubed and steamed until they are firm yet tender. Then they are paired with creamy plant-based ricotta, microgreens, refreshing mint, sweet Asian pear, tangy pomegranate, lightly candied walnuts and a bright balsamic vinaigrette for a salad that totally satisfies your taste buds.

To make the salad, slice the beets into ½-inch (1.3-cm) cubes and place them in a steamer basket. Set the steamer basket in a medium saucepan filled with 1 inch (2.5 cm) of water. Cover the saucepan with its lid and bring the water to a boil over high heat. Steam the beets for 15 minutes, until they are fork-tender. Transfer the beets to a medium bowl and set them aside to cool for 10 to 15 minutes.

Meanwhile, heat a small skillet over medium-low heat and add the walnuts. Toast the walnuts for 2 to 3 minutes, stirring them frequently, until they become fragrant. Add the maple syrup, salt and cinnamon. Cook the mixture for 4 to 5 minutes, stirring it frequently, until the maple syrup has thickened slightly and the walnuts are toasted. Transfer the candied walnuts to a piece of parchment paper and allow them to cool for 5 to 10 minutes. The maple syrup coating will harden as it cools.

To make the balsamic vinaigrette, combine the vinegar, tahini, mustard, maple syrup, lemon juice, salt and black pepper in a blender. Blend the ingredients for 30 seconds, until they are emulsified and smooth. Pour the vinaigrette over the beets and stir to coat them in the dressing.

To assemble the salads, use a rubber spatula to spread a layer of the Tofu Ricotta on four serving plates. Top the ricotta with some of the microgreens. Use a spoon to place the beets on top of the microgreens. Top the beets with the mint, Asian pear and pomegranate arils. Sprinkle each salad with the remaining microgreens. Garnish each serving with the candied walnuts and serve the salads.

## MOROCCAN CARROT SALAD WITH CITRUS–TURMERIC DRESSING

### Yields 4 servings

*If I could have only one salad for the rest of my life, this would be it. Eating the same salad for the rest of my days may sound repetitive, but it's so good that I just wouldn't carrot all! The carrot "noodles" are such a fun change from traditional salad greens. The carrots and other ingredients come together with the citrusy dressing to create the perfect balance of sweet, spicy, tangy and refreshing. The chickpeas and cashews provide an abundance of protein, which means this salad can be a hearty main or a delicious side to any dish.*

Salad

1 cup (146 g) raw cashews

1 lb (454 g) carrots

1 (14-oz [392-g]) can chickpeas, drained, aquafaba reserved

1 cup (174 g) pomegranate arils (about 1 large pomegranate)

½ cup (73 g) golden raisins

½ cup (67 g) roasted salted sunflower seeds

¼ cup (36 g) sesame seeds

½ cup (8 g) finely chopped fresh cilantro leaves

½ cup (46 g) finely chopped fresh mint

2 green onions, finely chopped

Citrus-Turmeric Dressing

¼ cup (60 ml) fresh or refrigerated orange juice

1 tbsp (15 ml) reserved aquafaba

Zest of 1 large lime

Juice of 1 large lime

3 tbsp (45 ml) red wine vinegar

1½ tbsp (23 ml) pure maple syrup, plus more as needed

1 tsp ground turmeric

½ tsp salt, plus more as needed

½ tsp black pepper, plus more as needed

½ tsp ground ginger

½ tsp ground cumin

1 tsp garlic powder

¼ tsp cayenne

¼ tsp ground cinnamon

To make the salad, preheat the oven to 350°F (177°C). Line a small baking sheet with parchment paper.

Spread the cashews on the prepared baking sheet. Roast the cashews for 8 to 12 minutes, checking them frequently during the final 5 minutes to make sure they are golden without being burned. Remove the cashews from the oven and set them aside to cool.

Meanwhile, use a julienne peeler to create "noodles" with each carrot. Place all of the carrot noodles in a large bowl that has a tight-fitting lid. Add the chickpeas, cashews, pomegranate arils, raisins, sunflower seeds, sesame seeds, cilantro, mint and green onions to the carrots. Use salad servers or tongs to combine the ingredients. Set the salad aside.

To make the citrus-turmeric dressing, combine the orange juice, aquafaba, lime zest, lime juice, vinegar, maple syrup, turmeric, salt, black pepper, ginger, cumin, garlic powder, cayenne and cinnamon in a blender. Blend the ingredients for 30 seconds, until the dressing is completely smooth. Taste the dressing and add more salt, black pepper and maple syrup if desired.

Pour the dressing over the salad. Cover the bowl with its lid and shake the bowl for 10 to 15 seconds to thoroughly coat the salad with the dressing. Chill the salad in the fridge for at least 30 minutes prior to serving it.

## Salad

1 large head cauliflower, cut into bite-sized florets

1 tbsp (15 ml) tamari, coconut aminos, Bragg Liquid Aminos or soy sauce

1 tbsp (11 g) nutritional yeast

1 tsp garlic powder

½ tsp black pepper

1 tsp salt

1 medium bunch fresh flat-leaf parsley, finely chopped

4 soft, pitted Medjool dates, finely chopped

¼ cup (34 g) roasted salted sunflower seeds

## Tahini Sauce

⅓ cup (80 ml) runny tahini

Juice of 1 large lemon, plus more as needed

½ tsp salt, plus more as needed

½ tsp garlic powder

4–6 tbsp (60–90 ml) cold water

# ROASTED CAULIFLOWER SALAD WITH DATES AND TAHINI SAUCE

## Yields 4 servings

A roasted vegetable salad is the perfect meal for any time of year, but it's especially delightful in the cooler months when you're craving a big bowl of veggies but also want something cozy and warm. This salad is both healthy and comforting. Savory roasted cauliflower florets meet tiny bits of sweet crystalized dates for a flavor explosion. The creamy tahini sauce is my go-to sauce for many things, and it complements this bowl perfectly.

To make the salad, preheat the oven to 425°F (218°C). Line a large baking sheet with parchment paper.

Place the cauliflower florets in a large bowl, and them drizzle them with the tamari. Use a large spoon or rubber spatula to gently stir the florets to coat them with the tamari. Sprinkle the florets with the nutritional yeast, garlic powder, black pepper and salt and gently stir them again to combine the ingredients. Spread the cauliflower florets on the prepared baking sheet. Roast the cauliflower for 25 minutes, until the edges of the florets are golden and crispy.

While the cauliflower is roasting, prepare the tahini sauce. In a medium jar, use a fork to whisk together the tahini, lemon juice, salt and garlic powder. Add 4 tablespoons (60 ml) of water and mix the ingredients together completely. Add up to 2 tablespoons (30 ml) of more water, until the desired consistency is reached. Taste the dressing and add more salt and lemon juice if desired.

Transfer the roasted cauliflower to a large bowl. Add the parsley, dates and sunflower seeds and stir to combine the ingredients. Divide the salad among four serving bowls. Drizzle each serving with the tahini sauce and serve the salads immediately.

## Salad

1 cup (192 g) green lentils

1 large bunch lacinato kale, stems removed, finely chopped

Juice of 1 large lemon

½ tsp cold-pressed olive oil

½ cup (90 g) pitted DIVINA® Frescatrano® or Castelvetrano olives, halved

¼ cup (14 g) bagged unmarinated sun-dried tomatoes, finely chopped

1 large shallot, thinly sliced

⅓ cup (48 g) Marcona almonds, coarsely chopped if desired

½ cup (30 g) finely chopped fresh flat-leaf parsley

## Lemon Pesto Vinaigrette

1 cup (24 g) loosely packed fresh basil leaves

¼ cup (15 g) fresh parsley leaves

¼ cup (34 g) pine nuts

¼ cup (44 g) nutritional yeast

½ tsp salt, plus more as needed

½ tsp black pepper, plus more as needed

2 tbsp (34 g) white miso

2 cloves garlic

Juice of 1 medium lemon

¼ cup (60 ml) red wine vinegar

1 tbsp (15 ml) pure maple syrup

# LEMON PESTO LENTIL SALAD WITH OLIVES AND SUN-DRIED TOMATOES

### Yields 4 servings

There is nothing better than fresh pesto: pesto flatbreads, pesto pasta, pesto-roasted veggies, you name it! So I thought, *Why not turn my favorite sauce into a vibrant, lemony vinaigrette?* I'm glad I did, because this pesto is the besto. It combines the garlicky, herby, umami flavor of pesto with the brightness of lemon juice and red wine vinegar for a perfectly balanced vinaigrette to top these tender lentils and veggies.

To make the salad, fill a medium saucepan two-thirds full with water and bring it to a boil over high heat. Add the lentils and reduce the heat to medium-low. Simmer the lentils for 12 to 15 minutes, until they are tender but not mushy. Drain the lentils and set them aside to cool completely.

Meanwhile, make the lemon pesto vinaigrette. In a blender, combine the basil, parsley, pine nuts, nutritional yeast, salt, black pepper, miso, garlic, lemon juice, vinegar and maple syrup. Taste the vinaigrette and season it with more salt and black pepper if needed. Set the vinaigrette aside.

To assemble the salad, combine the kale, lemon juice and oil in a large bowl. Massage the kale according to the instructions on page 80. Add the lentils, olives, sun-dried tomatoes, shallot, almonds and parsley. Toss the ingredients with salad servers to combine them. Drizzle the salad with the lemon pesto vinaigrette and toss the salad again. Chill the salad in the fridge for 20 to 30 minutes prior to serving it.

## Salad

1 (14-oz [392-g]) can chickpeas, drained

2 tsp (10 ml) coconut aminos, Bragg Liquid Aminos, soy sauce or tamari, divided

1½ tsp (9 g) salt, divided, plus more as needed

2½ tbsp (28 g) nutritional yeast, divided

1½ tsp (5 g) garlic powder, divided

12 oz (336 g) extra firm tofu, pressed (see Tip on page 32) and cut into 1" (2.5-cm) cubes

1 medium sweet potato, cut into 1" (2.5-cm) cubes

# CREAMY KALE CAESAR SALAD WITH CRISPY CHICKPEAS AND TOFU

### Yields 4 servings

How upset were you when you found out that traditional Caesar salad dressing is made with raw eggs, processed oils, cheese and pureed fish? On a scale from 1 to 10, I was a solid 9.65, and that was elevated to a full 10 when I discovered that the same salty, savory flavor we all know and love can be easily achieved with whole, plant-based ingredients. This recipe totally satisfies the Caesar salad craving with a deliciously creamy dressing, tender kale, protein-packed tofu and crispy chickpeas.

To make the salad, preheat the oven to 425°F (218°C). Line two large baking sheets with parchment paper.

While the oven is preheating, pour the drained chickpeas onto a clean kitchen towel and gently pat them dry. Transfer the dried chickpeas to a large bowl and drizzle them with 1 teaspoon of the coconut aminos. Shake the bowl to coat the chickpeas with the coconut aminos. Add ½ teaspoon of the salt, ½ tablespoon (6 g) of the nutritional yeast and ½ teaspoon of the garlic powder. Shake the bowl again to evenly coat the chickpeas with the seasonings. Spread the chickpeas onto one of the prepared baking sheets. Set the empty bowl aside. Roast the chickpeas for 40 minutes, until they are golden and crispy.

Meanwhile, place the tofu and sweet potato cubes in the bowl that held the chickpeas. Drizzle the tofu and sweet potato with the remaining 1 teaspoon of coconut aminos, and then use a rubber spatula to gently stir the cubes to coat them. Sprinkle the tofu and sweet potato with the remaining 1 teaspoon of salt, 1 tablespoon (11 g) of nutritional yeast and ½ teaspoon of the garlic powder. Gently stir the tofu and sweet potato again.

Carefully spread the tofu and sweet potato cubes on the second prepared baking sheet, spacing each cube at least 1 inch (2.5 cm) apart. Roast the tofu and sweet potato for 25 to 30 minutes, flipping the cubes once halfway through the roasting time, until the edges of the tofu and sweet potato are golden. Wipe out the bowl to use for preparing the kale.

(continued)

1 large bunch curly kale, stems removed, finely chopped

Juice of 1 large lemon

½ tsp cold-pressed olive oil

¼ cup (27 g) cauliflower bread crumbs or ¼ cup (21 g) almond meal

¼ cup (25 g) sliced almonds

### Caesar Dressing

2 tbsp (34 g) white miso

2 tbsp (30 ml) runny tahini

1 tsp Dijon mustard

Juice of 1½ large lemons

1 tbsp (11 g) nutritional yeast

1 tsp dried parsley

1 tsp garlic powder

½ tsp paprika

1 tsp pure maple syrup

Salt (optional)

Black pepper (optional)

While the tofu, sweet potatoes and chickpeas are roasting, combine the kale, lemon juice and oil in the bowl. Massage the kale according to the instructions on page 80. Set the bowl of kale aside.

Heat a small skillet over medium-low heat and add the cauliflower bread crumbs, remaining 1 tablespoon (11 g) of nutritional yeast, remaining ½ teaspoon of garlic powder and a pinch of salt. Toast the bread crumbs for 3 to 4 minutes, stirring them frequently, until they are golden and fragrant. Remove the skillet from the heat, transfer the bread crumbs to a small bowl and set it aside.

To make the Caesar dressing, combine the miso, tahini, mustard, lemon juice, nutritional yeast, parsley, garlic powder, paprika and maple syrup in a blender. Blend the ingredients until they are thoroughly combined. Taste the dressing and season it with the salt (if using) and black pepper (if using).

Pour the Caesar dressing over the kale and use salad servers to toss the kale with the dressing. Add the almonds, toasted bread crumbs, crispy chickpeas and tofu and sweet potato cubes. Toss the salad again to combine the ingredients. Serve the salad immediately.

# BALANCED BREAKFASTS

Breakfast being touted as the most important meal of the day means this chapter has big shoes to fill! If you're a new vegan, straying from a classic eggs-and-bacon breakfast or brunch can leave you feeling a little lost. This chapter is filled with recipes that will satisfy all of your breakfast desires with clean, nutrient-rich ingredients to help you power through each day. It also includes some fun and flavorful brunches to delight a table of guests over mimosas and Bloody Marys.

Whether you like a sweet or savory breakfast, this chapter has something egg-cellent for everyone (but hold the eggs, please). A hearty place to start is my Best Ever Tofu Scramble with Massaged Kale and Avocado (page 111). If you prefer to drink your breakfast, you can always find me drinking the Super Greens Detox Smoothie (page 112). And the Post-Workout Sweet Potato Recovery Bowl (page 115) is the perfect way to refuel your body after an intense morning workout. Feeling your best and nourishing your body starts with breaking your fast, and I can't wait for you to do so with these clean vegan breakfasts.

# POWER-PACKED BLUEBERRY PANCAKES

## Yields 12 pancakes

When you think of pancakes, you probably don't think of a power-packed, protein-rich breakfast. Traditional pancakes are made with processed grains, refined sugar and animal products, but this recipe is wholesome, cruelty-free *and* delicious.

These pancakes use a secret ingredient that may catch you off guard—silken tofu! But trust me when I say it works and results in what many of my friends and family members have declared to be the best pancakes ever. I can't help but agree. Not only do these pancakes have fabulous flavor and the perfect fluffy texture but they are also full of protein and nutrients, which means you really can have your pancake and eat it too.

### Pancakes

8 oz (224 g) silken tofu

1½ cups (360 ml) water

2½ cups (225 g) gluten-free rolled oats

3 tbsp (21 g) ground flaxseed

2 tbsp (30 ml) pure maple syrup

2 tsp (10 ml) pure vanilla extract

1 tbsp (15 ml) apple cider vinegar

1 tbsp (15 ml) fresh lemon juice

1½ tsp (8 g) baking powder

½ tsp baking soda

¼ tsp salt

½ tsp ground cinnamon

1 cup (148 g) fresh or frozen blueberries

Avocado oil spray

### For Serving

½ cup (120 ml) plain unsweetened coconut yogurt

½ cup (120 ml) pure maple syrup

½ cup (74 g) fresh blueberries

2 tbsp (20 g) hemp seeds

To make the pancakes, combine the tofu, water, oats, flaxseed, maple syrup, vanilla, vinegar, lemon juice, baking powder, baking soda, salt and cinnamon in a blender. Blend the ingredients at medium-high speed for 30 seconds, until the batter is smooth and creamy. Use a long wooden spoon or rubber spatula to gently fold the blueberries into the batter. Set the batter aside and let it rest for 5 minutes. The batter will thicken slightly as it sits.

Meanwhile, preheat the oven to 250°F (121°C) and place an ovenproof cooling rack on a large baking sheet.

Heat a large cast-iron skillet over low heat and spray it lightly with the avocado oil spray. Test the skillet to see if it is ready: Pour 1 tablespoon (15 ml) of the pancake batter in the skillet. Cook the mini pancake for 2 minutes, and then flip it and cook it on the opposite side for 2 minutes. If the skillet is evenly heated and ready, the mini pancake should cook evenly and flip easily. Enjoy this mini cake as a breakfast appetizer while you prepare the rest of the pancakes!

Use a ¼-cup (60-ml) scoop to pour batter into the skillet, making two or three pancakes at a time. Let the pancakes cook, undisturbed, for about 3 minutes, until small bubbles start to form on the top of the batter. Use a thin metal spatula to flip the pancakes, and then cook them for 2 minutes on the opposite side. Transfer the cooked pancakes to the cooling rack on the baking sheet and place the baking sheet in the oven to keep the pancakes warm. Repeat this process with the remaining batter, transferring each batch of pancakes to the oven to keep them warm.

Serve the pancakes in a tall stack topped with a dollop of the yogurt, a drizzle of the maple syrup, a few fresh blueberries and a sprinkle of hemp seeds.

½ cup (120 ml) plain unsweetened plant milk

¾ tsp kala namak

½ tsp black pepper

½ tsp paprika

½ tsp garlic powder

½ tsp onion powder

¼ tsp ground turmeric

2 tbsp (22 g) nutritional yeast

1 tbsp (6 g) chickpea flour

½ tsp arrowroot powder

Avocado oil spray, water or vegetable broth, as needed

14 oz (392 g) extra firm tofu, crumbled into bite-sized pieces

1 large bunch lacinato kale, stems removed, finely chopped

Juice of 1 small lemon

½ tsp cold-pressed olive oil

1 large avocado, thinly sliced, for serving

Hot sauce (optional)

# BEST EVER TOFU SCRAMBLE WITH MASSAGED KALE AND AVOCADO

## Yields 4 servings

Like many other vegans, when I first switched to a plant-based diet, I found that eggs were one of the hardest things to give up. Perfecting this egg-ceptional tofu scramble recipe made the transition much easier. I promise it's the only tofu scramble recipe you need. It's fluffy, eggy and ready in just fifteen minutes. It also has just as much protein and a similar number of calories as scrambled eggs, but far less cholesterol and sodium! This is the staple recipe I make whenever I want to incorporate tofu scramble into a dish like breakfast burritos, breakfast tacos or avocado toast.

In a small jar or bowl, use a fork to whisk together the milk, kala namak, black pepper, paprika, garlic powder, onion powder, turmeric, nutritional yeast, flour and arrowroot powder. Set the mixture aside.

Heat a large cast-iron skillet over medium-low heat. Lightly coat the bottom of the skillet with the avocado oil spray. Add the crumbled tofu and sauté it for 6 to 8 minutes, stirring it approximately every minute with a slanted wooden spoon or metal spatula, until the edges of the tofu become golden.

Pour the seasoning mixture into the skillet, immediately stirring to coat the tofu. Sauté the tofu for 2 to 3 minutes, stirring it as needed to prevent it from sticking.

While the tofu is cooking, combine the kale, lemon juice and olive oil in a large bowl. Massage the kale according to the instructions on page 80.

Divide the kale among four serving bowls and top it with the tofu scramble. Place the avocado on top of the tofu, top with hot sauce (if using) and serve the scramble immediately.

# SUPER GREENS DETOX SMOOTHIE

## Yields 2 servings

1½ cups (360 ml) water

Juice of 1 large lemon

1 tsp pure vanilla extract

2 tbsp (20 g) hemp seeds

2 tbsp (14 g) ground flaxseed

Pinch of salt

1" (2.5-cm) piece fresh ginger, peeled

1 soft, pitted Medjool date

¼ cup (23 g) fresh mint leaves

2 cups (60 g) baby spinach

2 large ribs celery, halved, plus more for optional garnish

2 Persian cucumbers

1 cup (140 g) frozen mango

1 large frozen banana

2 slices lemon, for garnish (optional)

One of the easiest and most delicious ways to consume an abundance of nutrients first thing in the morning is to start your day with a green smoothie. I start almost every day with this exact recipe and find myself feeling an immediate burst of energy and improved digestion—but most important, I enjoy every sip! The lemon and ginger are incredibly detoxifying, the hemp seeds and flaxseed are full of fiber and protein, and the fruits and veggies provide an abundance of nutrients. Greens have never tasted so good.

In a high-powered blender, combine the water, lemon juice, vanilla, hemp seeds, flaxseed, salt, ginger, date, mint, spinach, celery, cucumbers, mango and banana. Begin blending the ingredients at low speed and increase the blender's speed gradually as the ingredients begin to break down. Finish blending at medium-high speed for 20 to 30 seconds, until the mixture is totally smooth and creamy. Serve the smoothie immediately with an extra stalk of celery if desired and a slice of lemon (if using).

TIP: Following the order of ingredients listed in this recipe—liquids, lighter items like seeds and leafy greens, moderately heavy items like vegetables and very heavy items like frozen fruit—for every smoothie you make will result in an easier, smoother, quicker blend.

## POST-WORKOUT SWEET POTATO RECOVERY BOWL

### Yields 4 servings

This plant-powered bowl was made with athletes and fitness enthusiasts in mind. My dear friend was looking for the perfect breakfast to enjoy and aid in recovery after long runs and strength training, and this bowl fits the bill. It is loaded with whole grains and complex, high-quality carbs, making it the ideal fuel for your body after a workout. The quinoa, steel-cut oats and seeds are fabulous sources of complete plant protein to give your body strength for the day, while the sweet potato provides many vital nutrients, including potassium, to help your body on its road to recovery post-workout. Side note: No long runs or intense workouts are required to enjoy this bowl.

**Recovery Bowls**

2½ cups (600 ml) water

2 tsp (10 ml) pure vanilla extract

1 tbsp (16 g) creamy natural almond butter

2 tsp ground cinnamon, plus more as needed

½ tsp salt, plus more as needed

¼ tsp ground cloves

¼ tsp ground nutmeg

½ tsp ground allspice

½ tsp ground ginger

½ cup (81 g) gluten-free steel-cut oats

½ cup (85 g) white quinoa

2 cups (266 g) finely grated sweet potato (1 medium sweet potato)

2 tbsp (14 g) ground flaxseed

¼ cup (60 ml) pure maple syrup, plus more as needed

**For Serving**

½ cup (120 ml) plain unsweetened coconut yogurt

¼ cup (33 g) finely grated sweet potato (optional)

2 tbsp (20 g) toasted whole flaxseed

To make the recovery bowls, bring the water to a boil in a medium saucepan over high heat. Add in the vanilla, almond butter, cinnamon, salt, cloves, nutmeg, allspice and ginger, stirring the ingredients with a spoon to combine them. Add the oats, quinoa, sweet potato and ground flaxseed. Stir the ingredients and bring them to a boil. Reduce the heat to medium-low, cover the saucepan and simmer the mixture for 15 to 18 minutes, until the liquid has been absorbed and the oats and quinoa are fluffy and tender.

Remove the lid from the saucepan and stir in the maple syrup. Taste the mixture and add more salt, cinnamon or maple syrup if desired.

Serve the recovery bowls hot or cold topped with the yogurt, sweet potato (if using) and whole flaxseed.

## Chia Pudding

1¼ cups (300 ml) water

3 tbsp (45 ml) canned full-fat coconut milk

2–4 tbsp (30–60 ml) pure maple syrup, divided

1 tsp pure vanilla extract

2 tbsp (12 g) matcha powder

⅛ tsp salt

1 small yellow mango, peeled and coarsely chopped

¼ cup (40 g) chia seeds

¼ cup (40 g) hemp seeds

¼ cup (23 g) unsweetened shredded coconut

## Toasted Coconut Flakes

½ cup (60 g) coconut flakes

1 tsp pure maple syrup

Pinch of salt

## For Serving

½ cup (120 ml) plain unsweetened coconut yogurt

2 large kiwis, peeled and cubed

# TROPICAL MATCHA CHIA PUDDING WITH CREAMY YOGURT AND TOASTED COCONUT

## Yields 4 servings

This chia pudding is so creamy, flavorful and delicious it could almost be dessert. I love to make a big batch of this on Sundays and layer it with the toppings in Mason jars, so that I have easy grab-and-go breakfasts in the fridge all week long. The combination of tropical fruit and coconut will immediately transport you to the beach, and one of the best things about this breakfast—aside from mentally being on vacation with every bite—is the chia seeds, which are full of protein, omega-3, fiber and calcium.

To make the chia pudding, combine the water, coconut milk, 2 tablespoons (30 ml) of the maple syrup, vanilla, matcha, salt and mango in a blender. Blend the ingredients for 30 seconds, until they are smooth. Taste the mixture and add the remaining 2 tablespoons (30 ml) of maple syrup, 1 tablespoon (15 ml) at a time, if desired. Pour the mixture into a large jar, and then add the chia seeds, hemp seeds and shredded coconut. Stir the ingredients with a fork to combine them. Cover the jar with a tight-fitting lid and shake it vigorously a few times to make sure the chia pudding is well combined. Chill the chia pudding in the fridge for at least 30 minutes, or overnight. It will thicken as it chills.

To make the toasted coconut flakes, preheat the oven to 325°F (163°C). Line a medium baking sheet with parchment paper.

In a small bowl, toss the coconut flakes with the maple syrup and salt. Spread the coconut on the prepared baking sheet. Bake the coconut for 5 to 8 minutes, checking it frequently for doneness during the final 3 minutes to make sure it is golden and not burned. Remove the baking sheet from the oven and set it aside to allow the coconut to cool.

To serve the chia pudding, add a layer of the chia pudding to a small jar, followed by a layer of yogurt, followed by a second layer of chia pudding. Top the pudding with cubed kiwi and toasted coconut flakes.

If you'd like to make this chia pudding ahead of time, it will last for up to 5 days when stored in a Mason jar in the fridge. To keep the coconut flakes crispy, you'll want to add them right before enjoying.

## Granola

2 cups (240 g) unsweetened coconut flakes

½ cup (56 g) pecans, coarsely chopped

½ cup (50 g) sliced almonds

½ cup (73 g) raw cashews, coarsely chopped

½ cup (69 g) raw pumpkin seeds

¼ cup (40 g) hemp seeds

¼ cup (40 g) whole flaxseed

¼ cup (28 g) cacao nibs

1½ tbsp (21 g) coconut butter

¼ cup (60 ml) pure maple syrup

¼ tsp salt

½ tsp ground cinnamon

1½ tsp (8 ml) pure vanilla extract

½ tsp pure almond extract (optional)

¼ cup (36 g) golden raisins

¼ cup (23 g) dried goji berries

## Parfaits

2 cups (480 ml) plain unsweetened coconut yogurt

8 oz (224 g) fresh blueberries

8 oz (224 g) fresh raspberries

# HOMEMADE GRAIN-FREE GRANOLA AND BERRY PARFAITS

### Yields 8 servings

This recipe is a true gem. I was inspired to make it after realizing that most granola on the market is basically the nutritional equivalent of crushed cookies, with tons of sugar and processed carbs and very little protein or fiber. This granola is just the opposite—it is much more interesting and complex than traditional granola with an abundance of protein, healthy fats, vitamins, minerals and fiber. Here, the granola is layered with coconut yogurt and berries for power-packed parfaits, but it is also a great midafternoon snack and a tasty topping for oatmeal or chia pudding.

To make the granola, preheat the oven to 300°F (149°C). Line a large baking sheet with parchment paper.

In a large bowl, combine the coconut flakes, pecans, almonds, cashews, pumpkin seeds, hemp seeds, flaxseed and cacao nibs. Use a rubber spatula to combine the ingredients. Set the bowl aside.

In a small saucepan, combine the coconut butter, maple syrup, salt, cinnamon, vanilla and almond extract (if using). Bring the mixture to a boil over high heat and cook it for 3 to 4 minutes, stirring it constantly, until it has thickened slightly.

Pour the coconut butter mixture over the granola ingredients and use the rubber spatula to evenly coat the granola. Spread the granola on the prepared baking sheet. Bake the granola for 25 to 30 minutes, checking it frequently during the final 5 minutes of baking time, until it is golden.

Remove the granola from the oven and sprinkle the raisins and goji berries over it while it is still hot. Use a rubber spatula to gently stir the berries into the granola. It will still be fairly soft at this point. Set the granola aside for 10 to 15 minutes to cool and harden.

To make the parfaits, layer the yogurt, blueberries and raspberries in small jars. Top the berries with the granola right before serving the parfaits.

# TROPICAL PAPAYA NICE-CREAM BOWLS

## Yields 2 servings

2 cups (290 g) ripe papaya, cut into 1" (2.5-cm) cubes

1 cup (140 g) frozen mango

1 cup (150 g) frozen strawberries

1 large frozen banana

Juice of 2 medium limes

1 soft, pitted Medjool date

1 tbsp (15 ml) pure vanilla extract

1" (2.5-cm) piece fresh ginger, peeled

3 tbsp (21 g) ground flaxseed

3 tbsp (45 g) canned coconut cream

4 tbsp (60 ml) water (optional)

1 tbsp (6 g) unsweetened shredded coconut

2 tbsp (12 g) dried goji berries

2 tbsp (18 g) raw pumpkin seeds

2 tbsp (20 g) toasted whole golden flaxseed

4 slices lime, for decoration

Tropical nice-cream for breakfast? Yes, please! This ultra-thick smoothie bowl is so creamy and naturally sweet that it could easily pass as dessert, but it's so nutrient-rich that it's truly the perfect way to start the day. The berries and mango mean this breakfast dish is loaded with antioxidants, while the seeds add fiber and protein and the papaya provides powerful digestive enzymes.

Place two serving bowls in the freezer to chill. Doing so will help keep your nice-cream thick and frozen while you enjoy it.

In a high-powered blender or food processor, combine the papaya, mango, strawberries, banana, lime juice, date, vanilla, ginger, ground flaxseed and coconut cream. Blend the ingredients, stopping to scrape down the sides of the blender jar with a rubber spatula as needed; you can also use the blender's tamper to move the ingredients around. If you are using a high-powered blender or food processor, you should not need the water, but if your blender is struggling, add the water 1 tablespoon (15 ml) at a time to help thin out the mixture. Blend the mixture for 45 to 60 seconds, until it is thick, smooth and creamy, just like ice cream or sorbet.

Retrieve the serving bowls from the freezer and use a spoon or rubber spatula to fill each bowl with the nice-cream. Use the bottom of the spoon or the flat side of the spatula to smooth the top of the nice-cream. Top each bowl with a sprinkle of the coconut, goji berries, pumpkin seeds and whole flaxseed. Add the slices of lime purely for cuteness.

## STRAWBERRY, BANANA, ZUCCHINI AND OAT NOURISH BOWLS

### Yields 4 servings

If you haven't tried adding zucchini to your oats, you're truly missing out. It imparts a delightful creaminess, does not change the flavor and adds a lot of low-calorie volume to your bowl. This means you get to enjoy a bigger bowl of oats while secretly eating nutrient-dense veggies. Can I get a "Heck yeah"? I add zucchini to all of my oatmeal recipes, but this one in particular is a must-try. The combination of ripe strawberries and naturally sweet banana is the perfect flavor for this creamy oatmeal bowl, and the complex carbs, fiber and protein are a great way to start the day.

**Nourish Bowls**

2 cups (240 ml) water

1 tbsp (15 ml) pure vanilla extract

½ tsp salt

¾ cup (68 g) gluten-free rolled oats

½ cup (47 g) gluten-free oat bran

1 small zucchini, shredded

1 cup (166 g) coarsely chopped strawberries

1 medium banana, thinly sliced

1 tbsp (15 ml) fresh lemon juice

1 tbsp (15 ml) pure maple syrup, plus more as needed

½ cup (50 g) toasted walnuts, coarsely chopped

¼ cup (40 g) hemp seeds

**For Serving**

¼ cup (60 ml) plain unsweetened coconut yogurt

½ cup (83 g) thinly sliced strawberries

1 small banana, thinly sliced

Bring the water to a boil in a medium saucepan over high heat. Stir in the vanilla, salt and oats. Reduce the heat to low and simmer the oats for 3 to 4 minutes. Add the oat bran and cook the oats for 2 minutes, until they have thickened slightly. Stir in the zucchini, strawberries, banana, lemon juice, maple syrup, walnuts and hemp seeds.

Cook the oats for 2 minutes, until the zucchini and fruit begin to soften. Remove the saucepan from the heat and let the oats stand for 2 to 3 minutes. Taste the oats and add additional maple syrup if desired. Serve the nourish bowls hot or cold, topped with the yogurt, strawberries and banana.

Avocado oil spray

2 cups (180 g) plus 1 tbsp (6 g) gluten-free rolled oats, divided

1 tsp baking soda

1 tsp ground cinnamon

⅛ tsp cayenne

¾ tsp salt

1½ tsp (3 g) ground turmeric

3 tbsp (45 g) applesauce

1 cup (225 g) mashed ripe banana (2 large bananas)

¼ cup (60 ml) water

1 tbsp (7 g) ground flaxseed

¼ cup (60 ml) pure maple syrup

2 tsp (10 ml) pure vanilla extract

1 tbsp (14 g) minced fresh ginger

1 tbsp (15 ml) apple cider vinegar

1 large carrot, finely shredded

⅓ cup (48 g) golden raisins

⅓ cup (33 g) plus 1 tbsp (6 g) coarsely chopped walnuts, divided

# MORNING GLORY SUNSHINE MUFFINS

## Yields 12 muffins

You know how they say you make your own sunshine? Well, these muffins are a burst of sunshine in every bite with the bright flavors of ginger, turmeric, banana, carrot and walnuts. They are hearty and satisfying enough to power you through your morning—and they just happen to pair perfectly with a cup of coffee.

Preheat the oven to 350°F (177°C). Lightly spray a muffin pan with the avocado oil spray; alternatively, you can line the muffin pan with muffin liners.

In a blender, combine 2 cups (90 g) of the oats, the baking soda, cinnamon, cayenne, salt, turmeric, applesauce, banana, water, flaxseed, maple syrup, vanilla, ginger and vinegar. Blend the ingredients until they form a completely smooth batter. Make sure the ginger is fully blended. Use a spoon or rubber spatula to stir in the carrot, raisins and ⅓ cup (33 g) of the walnuts. Let the batter rest for 5 minutes.

Pour the batter into the prepared muffin pan, filling each cup three-quarters full. Divide the remaining 1 tablespoon (6 g) of oats and the remaining 1 tablespoon (6 g) of walnuts among the tops of the muffins, gently pressing the oats and walnuts down into the surface of the batter. Bake the muffins for 25 to 27 minutes, until an inserted toothpick into the center of a muffin comes out clean.

Allow the muffins to cool in the muffin pan for 10 minutes. If you did not use muffin liners, use a thin, sharp knife to loosen the edges of each muffin. Transfer the muffins to a cooling rack and allow them to cool completely. Alternatively, you can serve them warm right away.

8 oz (224 g) tempeh

1 tbsp (15 ml) balsamic vinegar

1 tbsp (16 g) tomato paste

1 tbsp (15 ml) coconut aminos, Bragg Liquid Aminos, soy sauce or tamari

1 tbsp (15 ml) pure maple syrup

½ tsp ground cumin

1 tsp chipotle chili powder

½ tsp garlic powder

½ tsp onion powder

Water, vegetable broth or avocado oil, as needed

1 large russet potato, cut into ½" (1.3-cm) cubes

1 large red bell pepper, diced

½ tsp salt

½ tsp black pepper

3 large leaves lacinato kale, spines removed, finely chopped

½ large avocado, thinly sliced, for serving

¼ cup (15 g) finely chopped fresh flat-leaf parsley, for serving

# SPICED POTATO AND TEMPEH VEGGIE HASH

## Yields 2 servings

A tempeh hash is like a tofu scramble's meatier cousin. This tempeh hash is filling, full of protein and makes a savory breakfast or brunch that will have you saying, "This is soy good!" Steaming your tempeh prior to marinating it helps it absorb flavor, but that step can be skipped if you're short on time.

Fill a medium saucepan with 1 inch (2.5 cm) of water and set it over high heat. Place a steamer basket in the saucepan, and then crumble the tempeh into bite-sized pieces over the steamer basket. Cover the steamer basket and saucepan with a lid. Steam the tempeh for 10 minutes.

While the tempeh is steaming, prepare a marinade by combining the vinegar, tomato paste, coconut aminos, maple syrup, cumin, chipotle chili powder, garlic powder and onion powder in a small bowl.

Remove the steamer basket from the saucepan and discard the water. Transfer the steamed tempeh to the bowl with the marinade and stir the tempeh to coat it. Set the tempeh aside to marinate for 5 minutes.

While the tempeh is marinating, heat a large cast-iron skillet over medium-low heat and lightly coat the bottom of the skillet with the water. Add the potato cubes in an even layer and cook them for 15 minutes, stirring them every 2 to 3 minutes to allow them to become crispy on each side. Add a bit more water as needed to deglaze the skillet.

Add the bell pepper to the skillet and sauté the mixture for 2 to 3 minutes. Add the tempeh and marinade. Stir the mixture to combine the ingredients. Sauté the mixture for 5 minutes, stirring it every minute or so, until the potato cubes are fork-tender, the bell pepper is soft and the tempeh is golden. Season with salt and pepper, then stir in the kale and cook the hash for 1 to 2 minutes, until the kale is tender.

Serve the hash hot in the skillet or in bowls, topped with the avocado and parsley.

## Almond Flour Crust

1⅓ cups (126 g) almond flour, plus more as needed

⅓ cup (48 g) tapioca flour

⅛ tsp salt

3 tbsp (21 g) ground flaxseed

⅓ cup (80 ml) water

## Spinach-Artichoke Filling

1½ cups (138 g) chickpea flour

1½ cups (360 ml) water

½ tsp baking powder

⅓ cup (80 ml) plain unsweetened coconut yogurt

1 tbsp (17 g) white miso

2 tbsp (22 g) nutritional yeast

½ tsp kala namak

½ tsp salt

½ tsp black pepper

½ tsp garlic powder

½ tsp dried parsley

½ tsp onion powder

½ tsp ground turmeric

½ cup (10 g) baby arugula, finely chopped

1 cup (30 g) baby spinach, finely chopped

½ cup (130 g) marinated artichokes, coarsely chopped

## For Serving

1 cup (149 g) cherry tomatoes, coarsely chopped

¼ cup (15 g) coarsely chopped fresh parsley leaves

# EGGLESS SPINACH–ARTICHOKE QUICHE WITH AN ALMOND FLOUR CRUST

### Yields 8 servings

When my husband, Clinton, and I traveled to Paris and the South of France for our wedding in 2019, we found that quiche was a staple dish at any brunch or breakfast table. I was inspired to replicate this French dish in a vegan, oil-free and gluten-free fashion that is sure to steal the show at any brunch affair. This recipe checks all the boxes—without any eggs, grains, butter or cheese. Believe it or not, it's just as delicious as the quiche we all know and love!

Preheat the oven to 375°F (191°C).

To make the almond flour crust, combine the almond flour, tapioca flour, salt, flaxseed and water in a large bowl. Use a fork to stir the ingredients until a dough forms.

Lightly dust a large piece of parchment paper with almond flour. Roll the dough into a ball and place it on top of the prepared parchment paper. Use your hands to flatten the dough into a disk shape. Dust the dough lightly with almond flour. Place a second sheet of parchment paper on top of the dough and use a rolling pin to roll it into a ⅛-inch (3-mm)-thick circle. Remove the top sheet of parchment paper and carefully flip the dough into a 9-inch (23-cm) metal tart pan. Use your hands to press the dough onto the bottom and up the sides of the tart pan, pinching off any excess hanging over the edges. Prebake the crust for 5 minutes.

While the crust is prebaking, make the spinach-artichoke filling. In a blender, combine the chickpea flour, water, baking powder, yogurt, miso, nutritional yeast, kala namak, salt, black pepper, garlic powder, parsley, onion powder and turmeric. Blend the ingredients for 30 seconds, until they are smooth and well combined. Stir in the arugula, spinach and artichokes. Pour the filling into the parbaked crust in an even layer. Bake the quiche for 20 to 23 minutes, until the filling is completely set.

Let the quiche cool for 5 minutes, and then slice it into eight pieces. Serve the quiche warm, topped with the tomatoes and parsley.

# GET UP AND GO SUPER SEED BREAD

### Yields 1 loaf (16 slices)

1½ cups (135 g) gluten-free rolled oats

¼ cup (40 g) whole flaxseed, plus more for topping

¼ cup (40 g) hemp seeds, plus more for topping

½ cup (56 g) finely chopped pecans

¼ cup (35 g) raw pumpkin seeds, plus more for topping

¼ cup (34 g) raw sunflower seeds, plus more for topping

¾ cup (84 g) ground flaxseed

1 tbsp (15 g) powdered psyllium husk

1 tsp salt

1 tbsp (15 ml) apple cider vinegar

2 cups (480 ml) water

There's nothing crumby about this hearty bread. In fact, there is a lot to love. Along with being delicious and seedy, it's filled with powerful fiber, plant protein and whole grains. The high fiber content is a great boost for your digestion and counterbalances the carbohydrates, so that they work in your favor. This hearty bread is delicious as breakfast with the Balsamic Fig Jam on page 75 or a smear of nut butter, and it can even be used for a sandwich at lunchtime!

Preheat the oven to 400°F (204°C) and line a 5 x 9-inch (13 x 23-cm) loaf pan with parchment paper, leaving enough paper hanging over the edges to lift the bread out later.

In a large bowl, use a rubber spatula to combine the oats, whole flaxseed, hemp seeds, pecans, pumpkin seeds, sunflower seeds, ground flaxseed, psyllium husk and salt. Stir in the vinegar and water with the spatula to create a dough. Let the dough rest for 5 minutes.

Transfer the dough to the prepared loaf pan. Use wet hands to gently form the dough into a loaf shape, and then sprinkle the loaf with more whole flaxseed, hemp seeds, pumpkin seeds and sunflower seeds if desired. Let the loaf rest for 5 more minutes in the pan.

Bake the bread for 60 to 65 minutes, until the loaf feels firm to the touch and is slightly golden. Lift the bread out of the pan using the edges of the parchment paper. Transfer the bread to a cooling rack and allow the loaf to cool for 15 minutes before slicing it.

Once the loaf has cooled completely, slice and store it loosely wrapped in a paper bag on the counter, or place it in a reusable Ziplock bag and store it in the freezer for up to 6 months. To serve the bread after freezing, simply pop each slice in the toaster or oven to reheat until lightly toasted.

# SINLESS SWEETS AND HEALTHY TREATS

Vegan, refined sugar-free, gluten-free baking—you heard me—that's what this chapter is all about. And believe me when I say these recipes do not skimp on flavor! Indulging in the finer things in life, such as dessert, is paramount—and this chapter was designed to give you a healthier, more balanced way of doing so without imposing restrictions. I wrote each recipe to satisfy each kind of sweet tooth: the chocolate lover, the berry lover, the peanut butter lover—you name it, it's in here. In these pages, you'll find a dessert for every craving and a recipe for every season.

Do not put this book down without bookmarking The Ultimate Fudgy Grain-Free Brownies on page 138 and the Chocolate-Dipped Coconut and Pecan Macaroons on page 151. I hope that as you prepare this collection of sweet and satisfying desserts you will find joy in every bite and that you will celebrate with me by making the No-Bake Vanilla Almond Party Bars on page 156. Desserts don't have to be filled with processed sugars, gluten and animal products, and I can't wait for you to experience how great you feel while enjoying every bite of these clean vegan treats.

## Almond Flour Shortbread Crust

Avocado oil spray

3 tbsp (42 g) coconut butter, melted

3 tbsp (45 ml) pure maple syrup

1 tbsp (6 g) lemon zest, plus more for garnish

½ tsp pure vanilla extract

2 cups (190 g) extrafine almond flour

¼ tsp salt

## Lemon-Ginger Filling

¾ cup (180 ml) fresh lemon juice

2 tbsp (12 g) lemon zest

2 tbsp (28 g) finely grated fresh ginger

1 (14-oz [420-ml]) can full-fat coconut milk

3 tbsp (24 g) arrowroot powder

2 tsp (8 g) agar-agar powder

¼ tsp salt

1 tsp pure vanilla extract

1 tsp ground turmeric

⅔ cup (160 ml) pure maple syrup

# LEMON-GINGER BARS WITH ALMOND FLOUR SHORTBREAD CRUST

## Yields 16 bars

When it comes to dessert, lemon bars are my main squeeze of the summer, and making a clean and vegan version of this ever-refreshing treat has never been easier. These bars are extra special with the addition of fresh ginger, and the almond flour shortbread crust is the perfect base for the tangy lemon-ginger filling.

To make the almond flour shortbread crust, preheat the oven to 350°F (177°C). Line an 8 x 8-inch (20 x 20-cm) baking pan with parchment paper, leaving enough excess paper hanging over the edges to easily remove the bars. Lightly spray the parchment paper with the avocado oil spray.

In a large bowl, use a fork to combine the coconut butter, maple syrup, lemon zest and vanilla. Add in the almond flour and salt and mix the ingredients with the fork until a dough forms. Roll the dough into a ball in the bowl. Use damp hands to press the dough into an even layer in the prepared baking pan, rewetting your hands as needed to prevent the dough from sticking. Press the dough with the underside of a metal spatula to create a completely smooth bottom crust. Use a fork to poke holes in the dough. Bake the crust for 15 minutes, or until the edges are golden.

While the crust is baking, make the lemon-ginger filling. In a medium saucepan, combine the lemon juice, lemon zest, ginger, coconut milk, arrowroot powder, agar-agar powder, salt, vanilla, turmeric and maple syrup. Bring the mixture to a boil over high heat, stirring it constantly. Reduce the heat to medium-low and bring the mixture to a strong simmer. Cook the mixture for 5 minutes, stirring it constantly, until it thickens slightly.

Pour the lemon filling into the crust in an even layer. Lightly tap the baking pan on the stovetop to release any air bubbles and help the filling settle. Allow the filling to cool at room temperature for about 45 minutes. Transfer the filled crust to the fridge to chill for 2 to 3 hours or overnight.

To serve, slice the dessert into 16 bars. Serve the bars chilled, garnished with extra lemon zest if desired.

½ cup (120 ml) pure maple syrup

⅓ cup (80 ml) runny tahini

2 tsp (10 ml) pure vanilla extract

2 cups (190 g) extrafine almond flour

2 tbsp (18 g) tapioca flour

1 tsp salt

½ tsp baking powder

⅓ cup (56 g) sugar-free vegan dark chocolate chips, plus more for topping

½ cup (56 g) toasted pecans, coarsely chopped, plus more for topping

1 tsp flaky sea salt

# SALTED CHOCOLATE CHIP PECAN–TAHINI COOKIES

## Yields 20 cookies

*Tahin-it may concern: These grain-free, naturally sweetened cookies are just as simple as they are delicious. They're made with very few ingredients and their bite-sized shape makes them a perfect treat for any time of day—for breakfast with coffee, an afternoon treat or a late-night dessert. The dark chocolate is paired with flaky sea salt for a satisfying sweet and salty experience.*

Preheat the oven to 350°F (177°C). Line a large baking sheet with parchment paper.

In a large bowl, beat together the maple syrup, tahini and vanilla with a handheld mixer for 15 to 30 seconds, until the ingredients are well combined. Add the almond flour, tapioca flour, salt and baking powder. Mix the ingredients at low speed for 15 to 30 seconds, until they are just combined. Use a rubber spatula to gently fold in the chocolate chips and pecans.

Use a 1-tablespoon (15-g) cookie scoop to place the balls of dough about 2 inches (5 cm) apart on the prepared baking sheet. Gently flatten each ball of dough and top it with extra chocolate chips and pecans if desired, gently pressing them into the surface of the dough. Sprinkle the cookies with the flaky sea salt.

Bake the cookies for 10 minutes. They will look a bit puffy and soft, but they will firm up as they cool. Allow the cookies to cool on the baking sheet for 5 to 10 minutes, and then transfer them to a cooling rack.

½ cup (96 g) coconut sugar

½ cup (120 ml) pure maple syrup

2 tbsp (14 g) ground flaxseed

½ cup (120 ml) water

⅓ cup (80 ml) runny tahini

¾ cup (173 g) mashed very ripe avocado (1 small avocado)

1 tbsp (15 ml) pure vanilla extract

1 tbsp (15 ml) balsamic vinegar

1 cup (95 g) extrafine almond flour

¾ cup (66 g) raw unsweetened cacao powder

2 tbsp (16 g) arrowroot powder

1 tbsp (6 g) espresso powder

½ tsp salt

¼ tsp baking soda

¾ cup (126 g) sugar-free vegan dark chocolate chips

# THE ULTIMATE FUDGY GRAIN-FREE BROWNIES

### Yields 16 brownies

The ultimate brownie should be fudgy, melt-in-your-mouth gooey and ultra-chocolaty. This combination is one of the finer things in life, and I haven't been able to perfect it without the use of excess oil or vegan butter—until now! These brownies are as gooey as they get, and you're going to absolutely love the surprise ingredients of avocado, balsamic vinegar and coffee—in fact, I bet you won't even be able to espresso how much you love them.

Preheat the oven to 325°F (163°C). Line an 8 x 8-inch (20 x 20-cm) baking pan with parchment paper, leaving enough paper hanging over each side to easily lift the brownies out of the pan.

In a large bowl, use a rubber spatula to thoroughly combine the sugar, maple syrup, flaxseed, water, tahini, avocado, vanilla and vinegar. Add the flour, cacao powder, arrowroot powder, espresso powder, salt and baking soda and mix the ingredients until they are fully incorporated. Scrape down the sides of the bowl, and then gently fold in the chocolate chips.

Use the spatula to help transfer the batter to the prepared baking pan. Bake the brownies for 32 to 35 minutes. Check the brownies frequently during the final 5 minutes by tapping on the center of the brownies. They should still be soft without being doughy.

Allow the brownies to cool in the pan for 10 to 15 minutes. Use the edges of the parchment paper to lift the brownies out of the pan and transfer them to a cooling rack. Allow the brownies to cool for 10 minutes before slicing them into 16 pieces.

## Crust and Crumb Topping

1 cup soft, pitted Medjool dates (about 10 large dates)

1 cup (90 g) gluten-free rolled oats

¾ cup (84 g) pecans, plus more for topping

1 tbsp (16 g) creamy natural cashew butter

1 tbsp (15 ml) water

½ tsp salt

¼ tsp ground cinnamon

¼ cup (23 g) gluten-free oat flour

## Cheesecake Filling

2 cups (292 g) raw cashews, soaked in hot water for 30 minutes or boiled for 10 minutes

¼ cup (60 g) canned coconut cream

2 tbsp (30 ml) melted coconut butter

3 tbsp (45 ml) fresh lemon juice

½ tsp salt

1 tsp pure vanilla extract

2 tbsp (30 ml) pure maple syrup

## Apple Pie Filling

1 large Honeycrisp or Pink Lady apple, peeled and finely chopped

¼ tsp salt

½ tsp ground cinnamon

1 tsp fresh lemon juice

1 tbsp (15 ml) water

½ tsp tapioca flour combined with 1 tsp warm water

# APPLE PIE CHEESECAKE BITES

### Yields 24 bites

The flavors of sweet apple pie meet the cool creaminess of cheesecake in a healthier plant-based combo of the two desserts. These no-bake bites are the perfect chilled summer treat and are a great make-ahead dessert to have on hand anytime your sweet tooth hits!

To make the crust and crumb topping, combine the dates, oats, pecans, cashew butter, water, salt, cinnamon and oat flour in a food processor. Process the ingredients until they are thoroughly combined. Set aside 1 cup (240 g) of the crust to use later as the crumb topping.

Press 1½ teaspoons (8 g) of the crust into the bottom of each well in a 24-well silicon mini muffin pan, creating an even, flat crust. Place the mini muffin pan in the freezer to chill while you prepare the cheesecake filling.

To make the cheesecake filling, combine the cashews, coconut cream, coconut butter, lemon juice, salt, vanilla and maple syrup in a high-powered blender. Blend the ingredients at high speed for 60 to 90 seconds, until the mixture is completely smooth. Remove the mini muffin pan from the freezer and, pouring the filling straight from the blender or using a spoon, fill each well three-quarters full. Place the mini muffin pan back in the freezer while you prepare the apple pie filling.

To make the apple pie filling, combine the apple, salt, cinnamon, lemon juice and water in a small saucepan over medium-high heat. Bring the mixture to a simmer and cook it for 5 to 7 minutes, until it has thickened. Add the tapioca flour–water mixture and stir the filling constantly for 30 to 60 seconds to achieve a perfect pie-filling consistency.

Remove the cheesecakes from the freezer and top each one with the apple pie filling. Crumble the reserved dough on top of each cheesecake. Sprinkle each cheesecake bite with additional pecans if desired. Lightly press on each cheesecake to make sure the crumble topping and pecans are secure.

Chill the cheesecake bites in the freezer for at least 2 hours, or overnight. Remove the cheesecake bites from the freezer 10 to 15 minutes prior to serving them.

Leftover cheesecake bites can be stored in an airtight container in the freezer for up to 6 months.

# CHOCOLATE, CHERRY AND HAZELNUT FUDGE BARS

### Yields 20 bars

2 cups (270 g) plus 2 tbsp (16 g) hazelnuts

1½ cups (240 g) plus 2 tbsp (20 g) unsweetened dried Bing cherries, divided

2 tbsp (28 g) coconut butter

½ cup (120 ml) pure maple syrup

¾ cup (66 g) unsweetened raw cacao powder

1 tbsp (15 ml) pure vanilla extract

1 tbsp (15 ml) pure almond extract

½ tsp salt

1–2 tbsp (15–30 ml) water (optional)

½ tsp flaky sea salt

Dense, chewy chocolate meets tart cherries, nutty hazelnuts and flaky sea salt for a decadent treat that tastes way too good to be healthy. Truth be told, this treat is made with whole-food ingredients that are anti-inflammatory and full of antioxidants, meaning these tasty bars are just as nutritious as they are delicious. Plus, they live in the freezer and can be stored for up to six months, so they're an easy make-ahead treat that is choc-full of fun.

Preheat the oven to 350°F (177°C). Line a small baking sheet with parchment paper, leaving some excess parchment paper hanging over the sides.

Spread the hazelnuts in an even layer on the prepared baking sheet. Roast the hazelnuts for 10 to 12 minutes, until they become slightly more bronze in color and fragrant—check on them frequently during the final 2 minutes to make sure they do not burn. Remove the hazelnuts from the oven, and then lift them from the baking sheet using the edges of the parchment paper. Set the hazelnuts aside to cool for 5 minutes.

While the hazelnuts are cooling, line a 9 x 9–inch (23 x 23–cm) baking pan with parchment paper, leaving excess parchment paper hanging over each side to easily remove the bars later on.

In a food processor, combine 2 cups (270 g) of the hazelnuts, 1½ cups (240 g) of the cherries, the coconut butter, maple syrup, cacao powder, vanilla, almond extract and salt. Process the ingredients at high speed until they are smooth and completely combined, stopping to scrape down the sides of the food processor's bowl with a rubber spatula as needed. Depending on the moisture level of your cherries, you may need to add the water to achieve the perfect consistency—the mixture should be stretchy and pliable but firm. Once this ideal texture is achieved, use the rubber spatula to transfer the mixture to the prepared baking pan. Use slightly damp hands to press the bar mixture into a smooth, even layer.

With a knife, coarsely chop the remaining 2 tablespoons (16 g) of hazelnuts and the remaining 2 tablespoons (20 g) of cherries. Sprinkle the hazelnuts and cherries on top of the bar mixture, and then sprinkle everything with the flaky sea salt. Gently press the toppings into the bar mixture with your hands or a spatula.

Place the bars in the freezer for at least 1 hour to allow them to firm up. Remove the bars from the freezer and slice them into 20 pieces or the size of your choosing. Serve the bars immediately or store them in an airtight container in the freezer for a ready-to-enjoy dessert, no thawing needed.

## Carrot Cake

Avocado oil spray

3 large carrots

⅓ cup (37 g) ground flaxseed

⅔ cup (172 g) creamy natural almond butter

1 tbsp (14 g) coconut butter or coconut oil, softened

¾ cup (84 g) pecans, divided

¾ cup (180 ml) pure maple syrup

½ cup (83 g) fresh or drained canned pineapple chunks

1 tbsp (15 ml) fresh lemon juice

1 tsp pure vanilla extract

2 cups (190 g) almond flour

½ cup (45 g) gluten-free oat flour

¼ cup (23 g) unsweetened shredded coconut (optional)

1 tsp salt

2 tsp (5 g) ground cinnamon

½ tsp ground ginger

½ tsp ground nutmeg

# NO-BAKE CARROT CAKE WITH CASHEW CREAM CHEESE FROSTING

## Yields 1 (9-inch [23-cm]) cake

As a kid, I never had much of a sweet tooth. I still don't—until it comes to carrot cake. In my world, carrot cake is the cake of all cakes. I love the moist texture, the spiced flavor and the cream cheese icing. Veganizing my favorite cake to create a healthier, whole-food, plant-based dessert is definitely one of my greatest accomplishments, and I can't wait for you to enjoy every bite. Like traditional carrot cake, it is at its very best after about 48 hours in the fridge, so I recommend making this cake two days in advance.

To make the carrot cake, lightly coat a 9-inch (23-cm) springform cake pan with the avocado oil spray. Alternatively, line a 9 x 9-inch (23 x 23-cm) baking pan with parchment paper.

Fit a food processor with the shredding attachment and S blade. Process the carrots to create finely shredded bits. Reserve 1 tablespoon (7 g) of the carrots to use as a garnish later.

Remove the food processor's shredding attachment, and then add the flaxseed, almond butter, coconut butter, ½ cup (56 g) of the pecans, maple syrup, pineapple, lemon juice and vanilla. Process the ingredients at high speed until they are well combined. Add the almond flour, oat flour, shredded coconut (if using), salt, cinnamon, ginger and nutmeg, and process the mixture at high speed until the ingredients are fully incorporated, stopping to scrape down the sides of the processor's bowl as needed.

Transfer the carrot cake batter to the prepared cake pan and use a rubber spatula to smooth it into an even layer. Place the carrot cake in the freezer to chill for about 15 minutes.

(continued)

Cashew Cream Cheese Frosting

1 cup (146 g) raw cashews, boiled for 10 minutes and cooled

Juice of ½ large lemon

⅛ tsp ground cinnamon

¼ tsp salt

2 tbsp (30 ml) water, plus more as needed

1 tsp pure vanilla extract

¼ cup (60 ml) pure maple syrup, plus more as needed

1 tbsp (14 g) coconut butter, melted

Meanwhile, prepare the cashew cream cheese frosting. In a high-powered blender, combine the cashews, lemon juice, cinnamon, salt, water, vanilla, maple syrup and coconut butter. Blend the ingredients for 1½ to 2 minutes, until a smooth and creamy frosting forms. Stop blending and scrape down the sides of the blender jar with a rubber spatula as needed. If your blender is struggling, add extra water 1 tablespoon (15 ml) at a time, but be sure that the frosting is not too thin—it should be thick and sturdy. Taste the frosting and add additional maple syrup if desired.

Remove the cake from the freezer. Use a rubber spatula to spread the frosting on the cake in an even layer. Coarsely chop the remaining ¼ cup (28 g) of pecans and sprinkle them along the outer edges of the cake, and then sprinkle the reserved carrots around the edges.

Place the frosted cake in the freezer to chill for at least 2 hours. Take the cake out of the freezer, remove the exterior ring of the springform pan and store the cake in the fridge. When you're ready to serve the cake, remove it from the fridge and slice it into 12 or 16 even pieces. This cake tastes best after about 48 hours in the fridge, and it can be stored in an airtight container in the fridge for up to 1 week.

## Cookie Crust

Avocado oil spray

½ cup (112 g) coconut butter, melted

½ cup (96 g) coconut sugar

¼ cup (60 ml) pure maple syrup

2 tsp (10 ml) pure vanilla extract

1 tsp pure almond extract

2 cups (180 g) gluten-free oat flour

¼ tsp ground cinnamon

½ tsp salt

1–2 tbsp (15–30 ml) water (optional)

½ cup (66 g) macadamia nuts, finely chopped

# SUMMER MIXED–BERRY PIE BARS

### Yields 25 bars

Heading to a summer barbecue? Make these light and refreshing bars! Each bite is bursting with sweet, juicy berries atop a chewy cookie crust for the perfect pie-inspired treat. Trust me, they're berry, berry good.

To make the cookie crust, preheat the oven to 350°F (177°C). Line an 8 x 8-inch (20 x 20-cm) baking pan with aluminum foil, leaving some excess foil hanging over the sides. Lightly coat the foil with the avocado oil spray.

In a large bowl, combine the coconut butter, sugar, maple syrup, vanilla and almond extract. Using a handheld mixer, mix the ingredients together at medium-high speed for 30 seconds, until they are fully combined. Add the flour, cinnamon and salt and mix the ingredients at low speed, until they are fully incorporated. If the dough is too dry or crumbly, add the water 1 tablespoon (15 ml) at a time and mix the dough until a soft, pliable texture is achieved.

Remove ⅔ cup (180 g) of the dough and set it aside. Use a rubber spatula to transfer the rest of the dough to the prepared baking pan, and then use your hands to press it into an even layer. For perfectly even bars, smooth the crust even more by pressing it with the backside of a metal spatula. Prebake the crust for 8 minutes, until it is slightly golden. Wipe out the bowl and set it aside.

(continued)

Berry Pie Filling

2 cups (296 g) fresh or thawed frozen blueberries

1 cup (123 g) fresh or thawed frozen raspberries

1 cup (144 g) fresh or thawed frozen blackberries

Zest of 1 large lemon

3 tbsp (45 ml) fresh lemon juice

1 tbsp (14 g) coconut butter, melted

⅔ cup (128 g) coconut sugar

1 tsp pure vanilla extract

½ tsp pure almond extract

¼ tsp salt

2 tbsp (16 g) arrowroot powder

While the crust is prebaking, prepare the berry pie filling. In a medium bowl, use a rubber spatula to gently combine the blueberries, raspberries and blackberries. Transfer 1 cup (148 g) of the berry mixture to the large bowl and use a potato masher or fork to mash the berries. Stir the lemon zest, lemon juice, coconut butter, sugar, vanilla, almond extract and salt into the mashed berries with a fork. Sprinkle the arrowroot powder over the remaining 3 cups (415 g) of the berry mixture and use the rubber spatula to gently coat the berries in the arrowroot powder. Pour the coated berries into the large bowl with the mashed berry mixture and use the rubber spatula to combine the ingredients.

Remove the prebaked crust from the oven and pour the berry mixture on top of the crust. Use the rubber spatula to spread the berry mixture into an even layer. Sprinkle the macadamia nuts on top of the berry mixture. Use your fingers to crumble the reserved dough into small pieces on top of the berries and macadamia nuts. Gently press the toppings down with your hands to secure them in the berry mixture. Bake the pie for 35 to 40 minutes, until the crumble topping is golden.

Remove the pie from the oven and let it cool in the baking pan for 15 minutes. Transfer the pie to the fridge to cool for at least 30 minutes. Grab the edges of the foil to remove the pie from the baking pan. Slice the pie into 25 bars.

Serve the pie bars right away or store them in the fridge for up to 5 days. Remove them from the fridge right before serving them chilled. Alternatively, if you prefer warm pie, you can reheat the bars in the microwave in 30-second intervals.

## Macaroons

1¼ cups (140 g) unsweetened shredded coconut

¾ cup (84 g) pecans

10 soft, pitted Medjool dates

½ tsp salt

1 tbsp (14 g) coconut butter, softened

1 tsp pure vanilla extract

2 tsp (10 ml) water

1 tsp flaky sea salt

## Chocolate Coating

½ cup (84 g) sugar-free vegan dark chocolate chips

½ tsp coconut butter

# CHOCOLATE–DIPPED COCONUT AND PECAN MACAROONS

## Yields 20 macaroons

At first blush, these macaroons may seem like any other coconut-date macaroon, but they are knock-your-socks-off good! Not only are they incredibly simple to make, but their sweet and salty flavor, combined with the rich dark chocolate, make them a total crowd-pleaser. I love making them for a bite-sized sweet treat at the end of a dinner party, and I often keep extra on hand to enjoy in the afternoon alongside a hot cup of coffee.

To make the macaroons, preheat the oven to 400°F (204°C). Line a large baking sheet with parchment paper.

Spread the coconut and pecans on the prepared baking sheet, keeping them separated. Bake the coconut and pecans for 4 to 5 minutes, until they are slightly golden. Check them frequently for doneness during the final minute to prevent the coconut from burning. Reserve 1 tablespoon (6 g) of the toasted coconut and set it aside.

Place the remaining toasted coconut and the pecans in a food processor. Set the baking sheet aside to cool, and replace the parchment paper if needed.

Add the dates, salt, coconut butter and vanilla to the food processor. Process the ingredients at high speed to combine them, stopping to scrape down the sides of the food processor's bowl with a rubber spatula as needed. Add the water 1 teaspoon at a time and pulse until the mixture begins to bind together and a doughy texture forms. The mixture should be fairly smooth but with notable flakes of coconut.

Once the baking sheet has cooled completely, use a 1-tablespoon (15-g) cookie scoop to scoop out a ball of dough and place it on the baking sheet. Flatten the dough ball slightly. Repeat this process with remaining dough until you have 20 macaroons.

To make the chocolate coating, combine the chocolate chips and coconut butter in a shallow microwave-safe dish. Microwave the chocolate and coconut butter at 50 percent power for 1½ to 2 minutes, stirring the mixture every 30 seconds, until a runny, melted consistency is achieved.

Dip the bottom of each macaroon in the melted chocolate and place them back on the baking sheet. Once you have dipped all of the macaroons, use a fork to drizzle the remaining melted chocolate on the tops of the macaroons. Immediately sprinkle the macaroons with the remaining toasted coconut and the flaky sea salt.

Chill the macaroons in the fridge for 15 minutes to allow the chocolate to solidify completely. Serve the macaroons immediately, or store them in an airtight container at room temperature for up to 1 week.

10 soft, pitted Medjool dates

1¼ cups (140 g) pecans

¾ cup (68 g) gluten-free rolled oats

¼ cup (23 g) gluten-free oat flour

¼ cup (28 g) ground flaxseed

1 tbsp (15 ml) pure vanilla extract

½ tsp ground cinnamon

Pinch of ground nutmeg

½ tsp salt

1–3 tbsp (15–45 ml) water

½ cup (61 g) unsweetened dried cranberries

1 cup (168 g) sugar-free vegan white chocolate chips

½ tsp coconut butter

# WHITE CHOCOLATE—COVERED OATMEAL CRAISIN® COOKIE DOUGH BITES

## Yields 24 bites

One of the best parts of being vegan is the fact that you can always eat the cookie dough. As a kid, I remember always trying to sneak bites of cookie dough when my mom wasn't looking—even though she warned me of the risk of salmonella, it was just too good not to take a bite! Little did I know that the same cookie dough flavor every kid craves could be easily replicated without the use of animal products and in a bite-sized healthy treat. These bites satisfy your child-inspired cookie dough craving using whole, healthy ingredients for a dessert you can feel good about enjoying.

Line a large baking sheet with parchment paper.

In a food processor, combine the dates, pecans, oats, oat flour, ground flaxseed, vanilla, cinnamon, nutmeg and salt. Process the ingredients at high speed for 30 to 60 seconds, until they are well combined, stopping to scrape down the sides of the food processor's bowl if needed. At this point, the mixture may be a bit crumbly. Depending on the moisture level of your dates, you may need to add the water 1 tablespoon (15 ml) at a time, securing the food processor's lid and processing at high speed after each addition, until a doughy texture is achieved. The mixture will transform from a crumbly texture to a ball of moist dough very suddenly. It should stick together without being wet or sticky to the touch.

Add the cranberries to the dough and pulse the food processor 6 to 8 times to combine the cranberries with the dough. Scoop out a 1½-tablespoon (23-g) ball of dough and roll it between your palms to achieve a perfectly smooth ball. Place the ball on the prepared baking sheet. Repeat this process until you have created 24 bite-sized balls.

In a small microwave-safe dish, combine the white chocolate chips and coconut butter. Microwave the white chocolate and coconut butter at 50 percent power for 1 to 1½ minutes, stopping every 30 seconds to stir the mixture, until they are completely melted.

Working with one cookie dough bite at a time, roll 12 of the bites in the white chocolate with a fork to fully coat them. Lift each bite out of the white chocolate with the fork, letting the excess white chocolate drip off of the bite. Return the coated bites to the prepared baking sheet. Use a fork to drizzle the remaining white chocolate over the remaining 12 bites.

Freeze the bites, still on the baking sheet, for 15 minutes to allow the white chocolate to fully solidify. Serve the bites immediately, or store them in an airtight container at room temperature for up to 1 week.

## Cookies

1 tbsp (7 g) ground flaxseed

3 tbsp (45 ml) water

1 tbsp (15 ml) pure vanilla extract

1 cup (258 g) creamy natural peanut butter

⅓ cup (80 ml) pure maple syrup

⅓ cup (64 g) coconut sugar

½ tsp salt

¾ tsp baking soda

## Chocolate-Peanut Coating

1 cup (168 g) sugar-free vegan dark chocolate chips

½ tsp coconut butter

¼ tsp flaky sea salt

¼ cup (36 g) roasted salted peanuts, coarsely chopped

# DARK CHOCOLATE–COVERED FLOURLESS PEANUT BUTTER COOKIES

## Yields 20 cookies

Peanut butter cookies are my most favorite type of cookie, and this recipe has the familiar chewy texture and sweet and salty flavor you know and love, but with only six ingredients and absolutely zero flour! Traditional peanut butter cookie recipes include eggs, butter, flour and refined sugar—and once you taste how good these cookies are, you will also be wondering why! For chocolate lovers, these cookies are delightful when dipped in melted chocolate as instructed; otherwise, they are also the perfect traditional peanut butter cookie.

To make the cookies, preheat the oven to 350°F (177°C). Line a large baking sheet with parchment paper.

In a large bowl, use a fork to whisk together the flaxseed and water. This will create a flax "egg." Let the mixture thicken for 10 minutes. Once the flax egg achieves a gelatinous consistency, add the vanilla, peanut butter, maple syrup, sugar, salt and baking soda. Use a handheld mixer to beat the ingredients at medium speed for 30 seconds, until they are fully combined. Use a rubber spatula to scrape down the sides of the bowl and mix the cookie dough again briefly if needed.

Use a 1½-tablespoon (23-g) cookie scoop to create 20 balls of cookie dough, placing each one on the prepared baking sheet. Use a wet fork to flatten each cookie dough ball and create a crosshatch pattern on top of each cookie.

Bake the cookies for 8 to 9 minutes. The cookies will look very light in color, underbaked and puffy, but they will firm up as they cool. Remove the cookies from the oven and allow them to cool on the baking sheet for 10 to 15 minutes, then transfer the cookies to a cooling rack and allow them to cool completely.

To make the chocolate-peanut coating, combine the chocolate chips and coconut butter in a small microwave-safe dish. Microwave the chocolate chips and coconut butter at 50 percent power for 1 to 1½ minutes, stirring the mixture every 30 seconds, until the chocolate is completely melted.

Dip half of each cookie in the chocolate, letting the excess drip off. Place the dipped cookie back on the baking sheet. Sprinkle the cookies with the flaky sea salt and chopped peanuts.

Chill the cookies, still on the baking sheet, in the fridge for 15 minutes to allow the chocolate to harden. Remove the cookies from the fridge and serve them immediately, or store them in an airtight container at room temperature for up to 1 week.

2 cups (292 g) raw cashews

1 cup (128 g) coconut flour

⅓ cup (80 ml) pure maple syrup

1 tbsp (15 ml) pure vanilla extract

2 tsp (10 ml) pure almond extract

2 tbsp (30 ml) water

½ tsp salt

3 tbsp (36 g) naturally colored sugar-free vegan sprinkles, divided

# NO-BAKE VANILLA ALMOND PARTY BARS

## Yields 16 bars

These bars are the last recipe in this book because, as they say, you should always save the best for last. They are also the perfect way to celebrate any occasion, and writing this book has been so fun and rewarding that finishing it definitely calls for a celebration. I hope that you'll raise a bar and cheer with me while enjoying this recipe—and all of the recipes in this book—on many special occasions. These bars are a party in your mouth, boasting the sweet flavors of vanilla and almond and amplifying the fun with colorful sprinkles to instantly make any event more festive. Cheers!

Line an 8 x 8-inch (20 x 20-cm) baking pan with parchment paper, leaving enough paper hanging over each side to easily remove the bars later.

In a food processor, combine the cashews, flour, maple syrup, vanilla, almond extract, water and salt. Process the ingredients at high speed until they are fully combined and a smooth dough has formed, stopping to scrape down the sides of the food processor's bowl with a rubber spatula as needed.

Remove the food processor's blade and add 2 tablespoons (24 g) of the sprinkles to the dough. Use a fork to incorporate the sprinkles into the dough. Transfer the dough to the prepared baking pan, using the rubber spatula to press down firmly to create an even layer of dough. For perfectly even bars, use the backside of a metal spatula to flatten the dough. Sprinkle the remaining 1 tablespoon (12 g) of sprinkles on top and press them down with your hands to secure them. Chill the dough in the fridge for 30 minutes.

Remove the dough from the fridge. Remove it from the baking pan by lifting the edges of the parchment paper. Transfer the dough to a cutting board and slice it into 16 bars. Serve the bars right away, or store them in an airtight container at room temperature or in the fridge for up to 1 week.

# ACKNOWLEDGMENTS

Ever since I started my blog, people have said to me, "You should write a book," and it has been a dream of mine since day one. Writing this book has been one of the most challenging and impactful experiences that I have had on my foodie journey. It has enabled me to grow in ways I never anticipated, and it forced me to push myself to new levels of creativity and precision in my recipe development, food styling and photography. I am beyond grateful for this opportunity and would not have been able to rise to the challenge without an incredible circle of support and love.

There are many people I would like to thank for their help, support and love along the way:

My loving husband, Clinton, for always supporting this dream of mine by allowing me the opportunity and being the biggest hype-man ever. Thank you for always sampling my recipes, even the experimental ones that didn't turn out great or the ones that had sweet potato (which we all know you don't love). I'm forever grateful for your support on countless cookbook shooting days, when you came home to a shockingly messy kitchen and never complained but immediately started helping with dishes. Thank you for being the best sous-chef a girl could ever want. This book could not have happened without you.

My parents, Bob and Diane, for instilling in me a deep love of cooking at a very young age. Thank you, Mom, for teaching me some of the best recipes and kitchen tips and tricks I know. Thank you, Dad, for introducing me to new foods, teaching me how to make the best breakfasts ever (which are usually at least two courses) and for always providing helpful feedback on my recipes. I wouldn't love cooking like I do if it weren't for the two of you.

My friends and family members—including David, Christine, Barbara, Don, Rachel, Michelle, Whitney, Eric, Jenny, Bryan, Megan, Nick, Ivy, Lon, Lynn, Alyssa, Robbie, Claire, Theo, Rachel, Ron, Sam, Kaylie, Seb, Bob, Bobbi, Natalie, April and Matt—who sampled dozens and dozens of recipes for this book and took the time to provide thoughtful and detailed feedback on each, making sure we got every single one perfect.

To my wonderful in-laws, for always being willing to try my new vegan recipe creations, for sharing new culinary experiences with me locally and internationally and for always being so thoughtful to prepare unique vegan meals when we come to visit. You both inspire me with your love of unique, international food!

To my incredibly brilliant, kind and beautiful friend, Jenny, for sharing your expertise as a registered dietitian, helping guide me as these recipes were written and being an incredible mentor.

To Megan, for helping me and supporting me with marketing questions, caption ideas, content concepts and more from day one. Thank you, too, for helping me come up with the name for my blog, Jackfruitful Kitchen, for always sampling recipes and for helping me shop for food-styling dishes, accessories and staging items for shooting this book. Thank you for preparing multiple recipes at home to make sure they were written "just right."

To my editor, Emily, and the entire Page Street Publishing team for finding me, believing in me and supporting my concept for this book. Thank you for making my vision come to life.

To my jackfruitfulkitchen Instagram followers, for supporting me, making my recipes, sharing my posts and telling your friends. And to my Instagram foodie fam for being such a profound resource and always being inclusive and supportive of each other. I am blown away by how amazing the plant-based food community is. I owe a big thank-you to @betterfoodguru, @healthysimpleyum, @plantedinthekitchen, @clairebear_bites, @janetsmunchmeals and @herbivoreskitchen, as well as the vegan pages @goodoldvegan, @veganbowls, @plantd.co, @forksoverknives and @meatlessmonday for sharing so many of my recipes and helping me reach new followers.

# ABOUT THE AUTHOR

Jackie Akerberg is the recipe creator, food lover and photographer behind the popular plant-based food blog Jackfruitful Kitchen and the Instagram account @jackfruitfulkitchen. What started as a creative outlet and passion project after Jackie went vegan in 2019 has turned into a much bigger part of Jackie's life, with a rapidly growing Internet presence and now her first cookbook. Jackie specializes in creating original, delicious, easy-to-follow vegan and gluten-free recipes to simplify healthy cooking and meal planning while utilizing whole foods and organic ingredients that are good for you and good for the planet. Jackie has been featured in *The Complete Guide to Plant-Based Food* and *dsm* magazine, Good Old Vegan and Vegan Bowls™.

When Jackie is not creating new recipes, photographing food and writing content, she is busy managing the daily operations and systems of the entrepreneurial world she shares with her husband, Clinton. This includes their wealth-management firm, their coworking space and a portfolio of real estate and Airbnb properties. Being self-employed enables Jackie and Clinton to travel often, which they love to do. Some of their favorite destinations are Paris, the South of France (where they were married), Colorado and the Caribbean. They love to enjoy new vegan food experiences, good wine, hiking, cycling, sailing, diving and skiing.

Jackie lives in Des Moines, Iowa, where she grew up, and she enjoys hosting dinners and parties for friends and family in her and Clinton's historic 100-year-old home. While she loves to travel, she also enjoys spending time in her rapidly growing hometown, where new restaurants are frequently opening with more and more offering healthy plant-based options.

# INDEX